DIGITAL TYPE DESIGN

for Branding

Designing Letters from Their Source

DIGITAL TYPE DESIGN
for Branding
Designing Letters from Their Source

Stephen Boss

CRC Press
Taylor & Francis Group
Boca Raton London New York

CRC Press is an imprint of the
Taylor & Francis Group, an **informa** business

A CHAPMAN & HALL BOOK

Table of Contents

FM	Introduction, map, cultures,	1
Chapter 1	A	8
Chapter 2	B	16
Chapter 3	C	22
Chapter 4	D	28
Chapter 5	E	34
Chapter 6	F	40
Chapter 7	G	46
Chapter 8	H	52
Chapter 9	I	58
Chapter 10	J	64
Chapter 11	K	70
Chapter 12	L	76
Chapter 13	M	82
Chapter 14	N	88
Chapter 15	O	94
Chapter 16	P	100
Chapter 17	Q	106
Chapter 18	R	112
Chapter 19	S	118
Chapter 20	T	124
Chapter 21	U	130
Chapter 22	V	136
Chapter 23	W	142
Chapter 24	X	148
Chapter 25	Y	154
Chapter 26	Z	160
Chapter 27	Letter Frequency	166
Chapter 28	Numerals	170
Chapter 29	Designskolen Kolding	178
Chapter 30	Interviews	187
Chapter 31	Glossary and Resources	211
Chapter 32	Bibliography	214

INTRODUCTION

Our modern alphabet is a collection of 26 glyphs or pictograms, and each one of these pictograms has a history, drawing on past Egyptian, early Semitic, Phoenician, Greek, Etruscan and Roman cultures. Many of our letters represent basic human needs and daily objects, ranging from water, housing, tools, architectural concepts and beasts of burden.

If North Africa and Phoenicia served as the incubator of our present day alphabet, Southern Europe served as its finishing school. Letters have been simplified throughout the ages, with every culture making changes; some simple, some dramatic, to each letterform. A number of our letters were added to our alphabet as time marched on, and most of these letters reside toward the end of our alphabet. Good examples are U, V and W.

As the cultures of Northern Europe, primarily English and Germanic, started using the alphabet, they created calligraphic variations which are known as blackletter. In blackletter, flourishes and exaggerated strokes are commonplace, with multiple extraneous strokes running parallel, rather than one single stroke. A blackletter M shows us the use of this multiple stroke approach. Additionally, note the vertical stroke running through the center of both the O and Q. Because of dramatic changes in stroke weight, blackletter highlights the pen nib as a driving element in many of our modern typefaces.

Etruria

Rome

Greece
Mainland & Islan

MEDITERRANEAN

The old adage goes, a picture is worth a thousand words, that is why I made a simple timeline with highlights of our alphabet. Earlier in the Introduction is an illustrated map showing the relevant regions of the Mediterranean that were instrumental in development of our letterforms. In the grand scheme of things, it is a rather small geographical region to play such a large role in the creation of the western alphabet.

Trade was the engine behind the proliferation of the Phoenician alphabet, similar to the way trade has influenced the use of English in present day international exchange.

Phoenicia

Egypt

The Egyptians

The Egyptian writing system, which used both ideograms and phonograms, inspired many of the early Phoenician letterforms, but unlike Phoenician letterforms, most hieroglyphs are representational of an object rather than a guttural sound. Egyptian phonograms on the other side represent sounds, while ideograms symbolize a concept or object. A number of these hieroglyphs were pared down and simplified by (and sometimes totally disassociated from) the Phoenicians to represent basic sounds.

The Phoenicians

The Phoenicians lived in now what is present day Lebanon, Israel and Syria and were instrumental in the development of our alphabet. Phoenician wanderlust for the maritime life and trade spread these pictograms throughout southern Europe including Greece and Italy. The Phoenician alphabet became an international standard during ancient history.

Stroke styles varied depending on the drawing tools and surfaces on which letterforms were drawn. For example, clay tablets of course didn't offer as much flexibility as papyrus. The Phoenicians began paying attention to the concept of line weight, their vertical and right leaning strokes were thicker than their horizontal and left leaning counterparts. This may have evolved from using multiple writing utensils and surfaces.

If you get the sense that you're dyslexic when looking at the ancient Phoenician alphabet, don't get too concerned, they wrote right to left. So many of our letters were flipped when introduced to Greeks and Romans.

Further into this book you will see some references to early Phoenician drawings which fall into three categories: Phoenician, Punic and Neo Punic. With the passing of time, you will note how the letterforms were simplified with modifications such as rotation, and deleting lines, along with many more variations which we will explore.

The Greeks

The Greeks began to pay attention to relationships, the amount of negative space each letter occupies, and how they related to each other. They also did quite a bit of renovation on the construction of numerous letterforms, deleting strokes and flipping characters.

These letterforms for the most part have a common height. Some drawing styles had a geographic flair particular to the area, but their names for each letter kept a strong resemblance to their Phoenician roots. For example, the Phoenician Pe was the Greek Pi.

The Etruscans/Romans

Etruscans from central western Italy spread North and South working their way into Corsica. They took the Greek alphabet and ran with it, keeping most of the Greek variation, and made simple changes. When the Etruscan grip on the region waned leaving room for the Romans to rise to power, things started changing again, including the alphabet. The Romans partook in streamlining the alphabet, yet again flipping letters to relate better with others, adding curvature and a touch of the Italian panache. As you will see, despite many updates and renovations, most of the letterforms' names have remained similar to their Phoenician originals.

Timeline

I made a simple timeline with highlights of our alphabet because, as the old adage goes, a picture is worth a thousand words. For the same reason, in the Introduction is an illustrated map showing the primary regions of the Mediterranean where major developments of our letterforms occurred. In the grand scheme of things, important developments in the evolution of our alphabet occurred within a rather small geographical area.

Trade has always been the driver behind not only the exchange of goods, but of ideas, language and culture. Commerce was the engine behind the proliferation of the Phoenician alphabet, much like English has become the lingua franca of international exchange today.

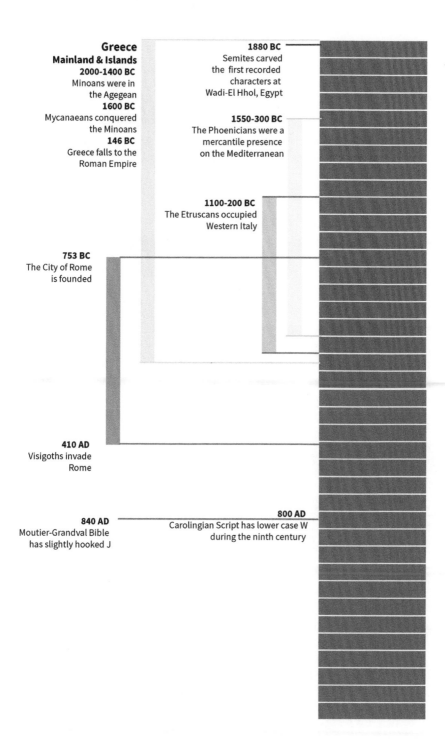

Greece
Mainland & Islands
2000-1400 BC
Minoans were in
the Agegean
1600 BC
Mycanaeans conquered
the Minoans
146 BC
Greece falls to the
Roman Empire

1880 BC
Semites carved
the first recorded
characters at
Wadi-El Hhol, Egypt

1550-300 BC
The Phoenicians were a
mercantile presence
on the Mediterranean

1100-200 BC
The Etruscans occupied
Western Italy

753 BC
The City of Rome
is founded

410 AD
Visigoths invade
Rome

840 AD
Moutier-Grandval Bible
has slightly hooked J

800 AD
Carolingian Script has lower case W
during the ninth century

A

A
Oxen

The A is one of the earliest letters, and has held its spot in first place for several thousand years. The letter's birthplace was Egypt, as a symbol for the ox, which was obviously held in high esteem by our ancient forebears. The Chinese had a special fondness for the ox evidenced by its inclusion in their Zodiac. The ox's characteristics include steadiness countered with a bit of stubbornness.

The early semites drew this character to look like an 8 with the top cut off. The Phoenicians, which called their version the Aleph, drew it in a similar way to our modern K. Eventually they transformed it to look much like our present-day A, except upside down and tilted to the right. In the diagram you can see the reference to the horns, head and ears.

When the Greeks got their hands on it, they renamed it the Alpha, and rotated it 180 degrees. They eventually pointed it upright to create the modern Alpha.

The Etruscans appropriated the Greek Alpha and kept it in unchanged. The Romans perfected the design adding geometry and visual corrections to the design.

The A is the second most used letter in the English language, so its roots as a draft animal are understandable. Now that we know that the A is derived from the ox's head, we can harness this energy. There are many options to work this energy into the letterform, ranging from weight, line quality, variation, slants and geometry. The A is one of the more common letters in the alphabet, and this workhorse of a letter's history has earned its employment in our modern usage.

The ox at times needs to be yoked so that it gets its job done correctly, so when drawing an A for a complete typeface, it has to get along with the other characters in the family. This means the relationship of the horizontal and angled strokes have to be similar to the other characters to be visually appealing. This limits the creativity of the designer a bit, but it aids in readability. On the other hand, if you are drawing an A for a logo or custom lettering you can remove the yoke and let the ox be more expressive.

The visual energy from the A is derived from the angled strokes, so when drawing this letter, think of the energy an ox exerts while plowing a field or carting a load. Even though the reference to an ox's head has been rotated 180 degrees, the energy still is completely directional. It moves your eye rapidly to the next letter form, so because of this, kerning becomes of utmost importance.

Drawing the A

The Greeks and Romans understood that the human eye had issues with lines, the lens tends to make columnar shapes pinch in their middle, flaring out at their tops and bottoms. To correct this they used Entasis to visually correct for this phenomena. Entasis adds a slight swelling to the column to visually correct for the issue. Type designers also use this approach to correct for the eye adding weight to stroke's intersection, for example, some designers would taper the point where the A's two angled strokes meet. Ink trapped typefaces show an extreme example of this.

It may be tough to make these tweaks if you are using a brush, nib, pastel or chalk, because the weight variations are achieved by pressure, the direction of the stroke and other variables. With most calligraphic letterforms, the weight variations are the most noticeable with rightward and leftward angles. Strokes leaning to the right tend to be heavier, and because of the downward motion and the angle of the pen's nib. Because of this, many noncalligraphic typefaces have developed with a similar weight variation. Times New Roman is a great example of this. If you're drawing vectors, these adjustments are made by the simple addition of Bezier points.

Times New Roman

center of cap height

- Note the relationship of the A to the E, especially in the placement of the A's hroizontal stroke or bar.
- In some designs, the diagonal strokes taper at the top or apex and flare at the bottom.

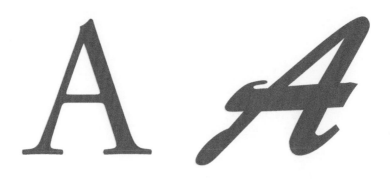

Humanist   Brush

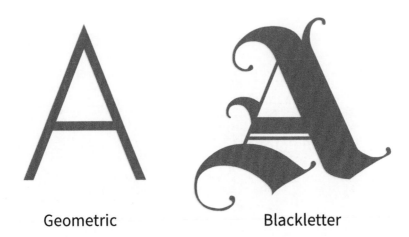

Geometric   Blackletter

The lowercase a has an interesting background. The variation that has the curved shoulder on the top and the bowl on the lower half came into existence in the late Roman period. It was a way to simplify the writing process. The French later created a version that looked like a lowercase c closed by a vertical stroke on the right.

B

EGYPTIAN

GREEK

EARLY GREEK

PHOENICIAN

ROMAN

B

The letter B's (formerly known as the Bayt) ancestors can also be traced back to Egypt. It was a glyph that represented shelter, as in housing. The idea of shelter was extremely important to the survival of our ancestors, it kept them out of the elements, and lent a degree of safety to their very existence. Many ancient cities that have the prefix "Beth" were named after housing, such as Bethel and Bethlehem.

The early Semites didn't change the B much from the Egyptian design, but as the letter passed on to the Phoenicians, some changes occurred. They closed the shape up and angled the block shape, adding a left pointing angle to the design.

The early Greeks retooled the Bayt into their Beta by bending the slanted stroke to create the double arched side of the Beta. The Greeks eventually created a flipped version, for the purpose of writing from left to right.

The Etruscans used the right reading Beta, but once in the Roman's hands, it had a facelift. The Romans visually corrected the B with minor tweaks, such as extending the bottom curve beyond the upper.

Drawing the B

It should comes as no surprise that the B's foundation reflects our ancestor's domiciles. The B has an almost structural feel to it, reminiscent of an architect's floorplan. I visualize a two-story building with bay windows. In my opinion, the B is one of the more difficult letters to draw, as it has a lot of geometry packed into one letter.

The B is not one of English's most commonly used letters, being the 17th most commonly used letter in the English language.

The Romans added a touch of Entasis to correct the letter-form for a visual sag. The lower bowl of the B extends a hair to the right more than the upper bowl. The cross bar is not equal to two of the curved strokes, but rather it is thinned out so as to not look so dense.

Typefaces like Times New Roman mimic the effect of a pen's nib, the top and bottom of each bowl is thinner, showing the stress and angle of the nib, while the thicker section of the bowl reflects the downward motion where the nib's full width is in contact with the surface.

Times New Roman

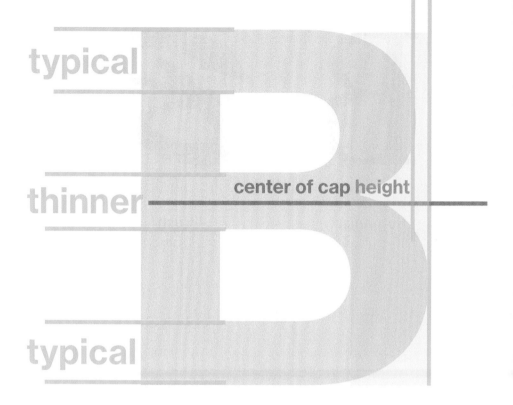

typical

thinner   center of cap height

typical

- Extend the lower counter's right side slightly beyond the width of the top.

- Note how the center stroke is slightly narrowor in this design, Neue Haas Grotesk.

B
Humanist

B
Brush

B
Geometric

B
Blackletter

The lowercase b was first used in Latin in roughly 500. The writers eliminated the upper bowl to speed up the writing process. This glyph made its way from script to modern day typeface design.

C

PHOENICIAN   GREEK   ETRUSCAN

ROMAN

C

Many in the past believed that the C was representational of our early ancestor's transportation, namely the camel, but that idea has been left in the dust. Now most agree that the C or Gimel was a throwing stick. The C and G are both cut from the same cloth. The C (as in clock) and the G (as in game) both have similar sounds. The C just has a bit more of a crack than the G does.

As mentioned, the Phoenicians called this letter combo the Gimel, and their pictogram looks like a crude 1. The Greeks eventually simplified the shape by adding curvature, to design a letter that was akin to the left parenthesis.

The Etruscans took the Greek letter verbatim, then once again, the Romans worked their magic and created the modern C by utilizing geometry in their circular design.

The C has the potential to give any word in text or a logo visual kick. The visual motion created by the curvature moves your eye directly to the next letterform, and the negative space in the interior aperture can aid in reading when paired with a more vertical glyph like an H or U. When mixed with an O, attention should be paid to the letter spacing or kerning so that the combination reads as one word rather than two.

Drawing the C

Perhaps the C's history as a throwing stick worked its way to Australia and evolved into a boomerang. It seems that a throwing stick can sling your eye forward in a line of text.

The C highlights the difference between a calligraphic design and a simplified monoweight design. The classification of Humanist typefaces is a great example of this. You should note how the pen's stress greatly affects the character's thick and thin variations. These variations give the letterform a visual rhythm, moving the eye along the page.

Monoweight typefaces on the other hand avoid the weight variations, creating shapes that rely on geometry to create the visual rhythm. There may be a slight change in weight within a single letter, but the difference is minimal compared to a Humanist glyph.

Brush lettering, on the other hand, captures the energy of the designer, the pressure of their hand, the charge (or the amount of ink) of their brush, and the movement of their hand. This gives more dynamism to line quality.

vertical stem

center of cap height

- The lower right part of the letterform extends slightly beyond the point that would create a perfect circle.
- The top of the C (as with all curved letters) slightly extends above the cap height and below the baseline.
- The stress of the letter, or its thinnest stroke weight, is on the top and bottom.

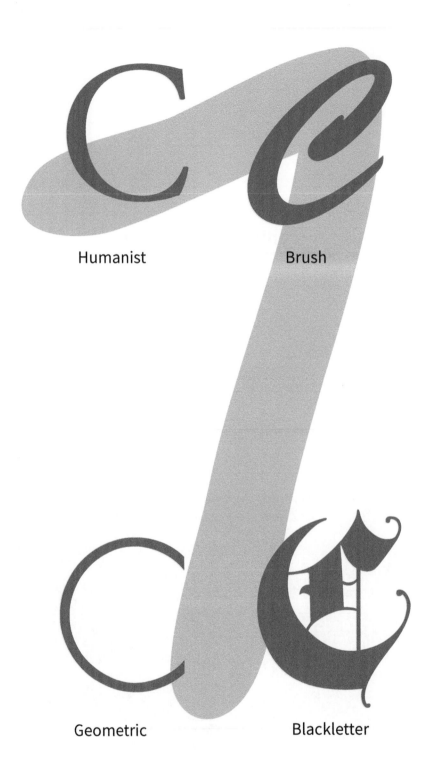

Humanist

Brush

Geometric

Blackletter

The lowercase c has an interesting background. The variation that has the curved shoulder on the top and the bowl on the lower half came into existence in the late Roman period. It was a way to simplify the writing process. The French later created a version that looked like a lowercase c closed by a vertical stroke on the right.

D

PHOENICIAN

EARLY GREEK

GREEK

ETRUSCAN & ROMAN

D

Our ancestors drew the D as a representation of a door or gate. This idea of a gate or door, similar to the B's architectural roots, surely represents the protective quality of a barrier which keeps thieves and wild animals out and your domacile, belongings and self safe.

The Phoenicians called their version of the D a Daleth, which meant door (and in Hebrew gate). They drew their Daleth to look like the upper right section of a crude semi-circle. There is a little mystery around the origins of the D, some ancient Serabit scripts have an illustrated letterform that resembles a fish, which may have been called a Dag, and perhaps the Dag morphed into the Phoenician Daleth.

The Greeks took the Daleth as the foundation for their letter Delta. Originally the Delta read from right to left, but they eventually flipped it to make a right reading version. The Etruscans used the right reading Delta, and passed it on to the Romans, who tweaked the geometry to create a modern D that is more appealing to the eye.

Drawing the D

The D's essence comes from its curved bowl, which was a design tweak made by the Greeks and perfected by the Romans. The present day letter doesn't resemble the original Daleth or "door." The original Greek Delta resembled the Phoenician's, but they flipped it because the Greeks flipped it and eventually softened the angular quality of the Phoenician's. The D isn't one of our most commonly used letters, it ranks just a bit under 4% in frequency of use, but it offers a dynamic presence in a word.

You should take note of the calligraphic line quality in a Humanist or old style typeface. The weight diminishes as the upper and lower curvatures intersect with the vertical stem. When drawing a classical humanist D the weight at the letter's widest point should also be the thickest part of the curve. Also, you can visually correct with entasis by thinning out the curved stroke when it intersects with the vertical stem.

A monoweight or geometric D may also have a slight deviation in stroke weight, to avoid density in its corners, but for the most part, the weights are quite uniform. Futura is an excellent example of a monoweight face. Rendering a D with a brush can add a lot of energy to your typography, the curved bowl moving your eye to the right with both upward and downward sweeps. You may want to try a few gestural strokes to get warmed up before you commit to your final product.

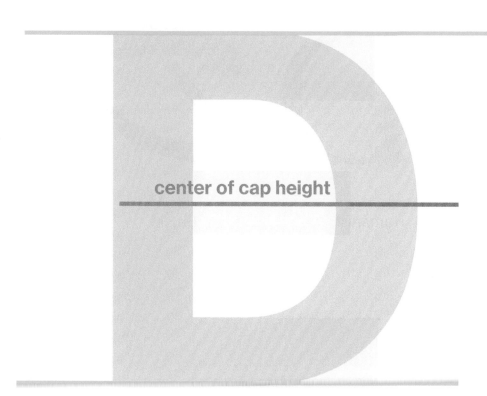

center of cap height

• Use your common vertical stem.

• Note the relationshhip to the uppercase E's horizontal strokes
• Because the curved stroke meets at a 90 degree angle, there is no need to enlarge the character.

Humanist

Brush

Geometric

Blackletter

The lowercase d was also first penned in Latin text in the 500s. The driving force behind this design was simplification. The scribes wanted to simplify the lowercase glyph into a single pen stroke.

E

SEMITIC

 PHOENICIAN

EARLY GREEK

 EARLY ROMAN

 ETRUSCAN & ROMAN

E

The E is an interesting letterform, and one of my personal favorites. My typography teacher, Richard Isabell, always encouraged us to use the E as the starting point to set up the relationship of the uppercase to the lowercase.

The three vertical strokes create open negative space, with a forward motion. The iconic FedEx logo harnesses that energy with their arrow hidden in the negative space between the E and x letter combination.

Most agree that the modern E was originally an Egyptian pictogram symbolizing a figure raising its arms to the sky. The Phoenicians name this letter He. The sound and its visual representation obviously changed a bit to lose the h sound but still remained close to its original sound. The Phoenicians began paring down the shape, cutting most of its human qualities, and rotated it counterclockwise. Their shape looked like a backward E with the vertical stroke extending below the lower horizontal stroke.

The Greeks kept the Phoenician version, and renamed it Epsilon, and passed it along to the Etruscans. The Romans perked up its geometry, flipped it and clipped the tail.

Drawing the E

I find it interesting that the E is a figurative letterform, being that I often begin an alphabet by drawing the E. My typography instructor, Richard Isbell, urged us to begin the design process by developing the letter E. This sets the tone and relationship between the upper and lowercase, and many other characters such as the B, F, P and R. The E is the most frequently used letter in the English alphabet, so its design is an important character in your typeface.

Creating an E with a brush or pen can add a lot of energy to your typography. Some calligraphic E's have a backwards 3 quality (illustrated below). In certain variations of blackletter, the vertical stroke is replaced by a semicircle akin to the uppercase C.

typical

thinner

center of cap height

typical

- The horizontal arms or strokes are slightly thicker than the B's.
  Some designs extend the lower horizontal stroke a hair wider than the upper stroke.
- The width of the horizontal strokes vary, the top stroke traditionally is the second widest, the center stroke is the shortest while the bottom stroke is the widest. This visually corrects the letterform, so it doesn't look top heavy.
- Note how the negative space is slightly larger in the lower section of the letterform than the top.

Humanist

Brush

Geometric

Blackletter

Latin manuscripts from the 450s display the first iteration of our modern lowercase e. The initially designed top wasn't a completely closed shape; that came later in the 500s.

F

PHOENICIAN   EARLY GREEK   ETRUSCAN

ROMAN

F
You Nailed It

The F is an interesting letter, it so closely resembles the E, but it is a consanant rather than a vowel. The sound we make to represent the F comes more from our lower lips rather than our tongues or rear throats.

The Phoenician name for F is very different than our modern day letter. They called it the Waw, which is depicted by a graphic of a nail or peg. The Waw looked very similar to our present day Y. I would suppose that the concept of a nail or peg must have been very useful to our ancestors, it allowed them to construct dwellings, furniture and primitive vehicles. So, that being said, I don't find it unusual that this item would spin off a letterform.

When the Greeks designed their version, the Digamma, they went back to the drawing board and discarded the Phoenician's design. The Greek version looked similar to their Epsilon (E), sans the lower horizontal stroke. As with other letters, the Greeks made a right reading version, too. The Etruscans once again used the Digamma, with minimal changes. When the Romans adopted the letter, they squared off the strokes to create our modern F.

Drawing the F

The F has very close ties to the E, both in placement of our alphabet and the overall look of the character. Knowing that the F's origins are totally unique from the E's may give us a new twist on drawing the letter. The F shares the upper extremities of the E, but that is where the similarities end. According to the Oxford Dictionaries, the F is the 18th most frequently used letterform in the English alphabet.

One of the great features of the F, in my opinion, is its ability to cozy up to the character to its right. The F's shape and abundance of negative space give it the ability to kern very pleasantly against most lowercase letters, and many uppercase letters, too. Drawing an F with a looser tool, again such as a brush or nib, can create forward motion, which moves the reader's eye rapidly through your word, logo or lettering.

typical

thinner

center of cap height

- Note how the center stroke or arm is slightly lower than the E's.

- The width of the top horizontal stroke is slightly wider than the length of the second horizontal stroke.

- Taper the strokes' weight where the two horizontal strokes intersect with the vertical stem.

Humanist

Brush

Geometric

Blackletter

The f like so many of our lowercase letterforms was designed by Latin scribes in the 500s. Speed was the objective like the lowercase letters before it. The scripts wanted to simplify the shape into two quick pen strokes. This character too carried over into modern-day European type design.

G
I Ⅼ G

ETRUSCAN **EARLY ROMAN** **ROMAN**

G

As mentioned earlier, the C and G both share a common ancestor, which is the Gimel, or throwing stick. The Greeks took the Phoenician Gimel, and in turn called it the Gamma, and the Gamma represented the strong sound of the G, as in game and graphic.

The Etruscans had no hard G sounds in their language, so they skipped on the Gamma. The Romans, on the other hand, needed a letter for their G sound. They took the C and added the vertical stroke to create a difference between the two.

Drawing the G

Now that we know that the G is a twin to the C, we can recycle what you created for the C in the design process of the G. Many typestyles treat the G's spur in different ways. A grotesque typeface terminates the circular shape with an arrow-like stroke. In the geometric camp, in typefaces like Futura, the G terminates with a simple horizontal bar.

Rendering a G with a brush or nib gives you a little more flexibility when terminating the G. A good example is seen in the typeface Mistral. Note how the G terminates with an aggressive downward pointing spike, while in a calligraphic face like Lucida, the G adds a flourish that tucks under the large portion of the letterform.

vertical stem

center of cap height

G

- The lower right part of the letterform extends slightly beyond the point that would create a perfect circle.

- The top of the G (as with all curved letters) slightly extends above the cap height and below the baseline.

- The stress of the letter, or its thinnest stroke weight, is on the top and bottom.

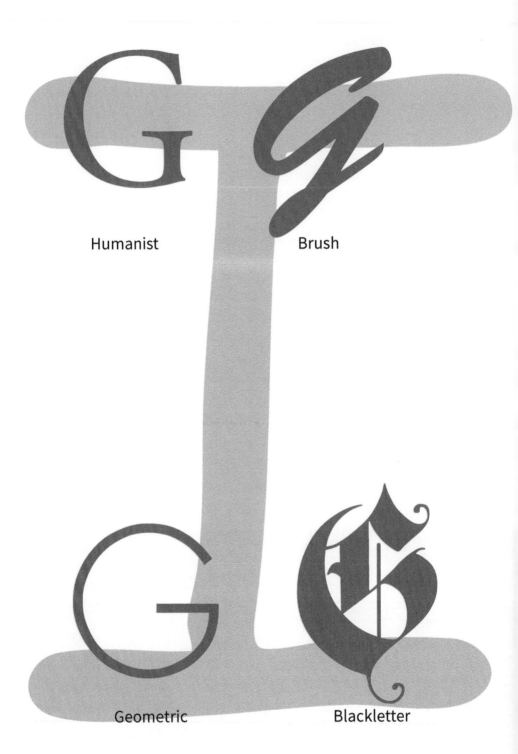

Humanist

Brush

Geometric

Blackletter

The lowercase g is a little more involved than the other glyphs before it. The initial lowercase letter was a simplification of the uppercase character, and it was drawn in Latin manuscripts from the 450s. This form became a two-storied lowercase g, used in popular French and English designs. The g with a single bowl and a terminal was first used in the early twentieth century.

H

EARLY PHOENICIAN   PHOENICIAN   EARLY GREEK

H

LATER GREEK & ROMAN

H

The H represents a hissing sound made by forcing air through the back of our throats. Think of words like help, hooray and hello. The H is one of the few letters whose negative space is open to both its top and bottom, in my opinion, this adds some visual stability. I view the H as a building block.

As you've read, our letterforms come from a wide range of pictograms, from livestock to housing. The H is no different. This letter is Semitic in roots and the Phoenicians called it the Het, and some say Khet, but most concur that this letter started off as a pictogram for a section of fence. Perhaps keeping tabs on your property, such as livestock, was enough to inspire a letterform.

The Phoenicians drew the Het by creating two vertical strokes, and connected the two with three horizontal strokes. The Greeks took this letter and tightened it up a bit to create their Heta. The Heta was tweaked to represent more of a perfect box with a central horizontal stroke. The early Romans adopted this boxy letter, both the Greeks and Romans eventually cut the top and bottom horizontal strokes, leaving us with the present day H.

Drawing the H

While building your typeface, logo or lettering, keep in mind that the H's roots are in fencing. The horizontal stroke is set up by the E, so you can see how each letter has a relationship with other letters in the alphabet. Once again, according to Oxford, the H is the 15th most commonly used letter in the English alphabet.

Drawing an H is one of the easier letters in our alphabet. You can use a common vertical stem used in your F, L and E and allow the E's center stroke to determine the placement of the H's crossbar. Some typeface designs taper the intersections of the two stems with the horizontal bar.

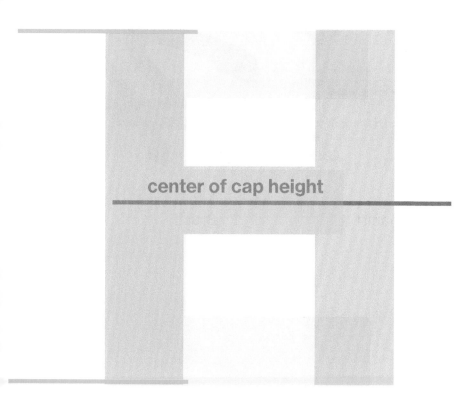

center of cap height

- Obviously, the H shouldn't be wider than the M.
- The vertical stroke may be a bit thinner than the horizontal stroke or bar.

Humanist

Brush

Geometric

Blackletter

The first version of the lowercase h was seen in England in the 700s, and was adopted by other Europeans and was later refined in the 800s. It appears as if the upper half of the right vertical stroke was removed for speed.

PHOENICIAN   EARLY GREEK   GREEK

ETRUSCAN & ROMAN

I

The I's Have It

The I is our most simplistic letterform, its stroke's singularity matches up with our notion of I, as in me, myself and I. It is represented by a sound, which like many others comes from the back of the throat, created by a sharp burst of air.

I find the origins of the letter I very interesting, and somewhat unexpected. The Phoenicians called this letter Yod or Yodh, which is symbolic for the human arm and hand. Their original glyph resembled a backwards F with a right pointing hook on the bottom. I assume the arm and hand could symbolize hugging, working, eating and many of our daily chores.

The Yod inspired the Greek's first stab at the Iota, it resembled a Z, with a fair amount of vertical stretch. The Greeks eventually simplified the Iota to be one vertical stroke. When the Romans got their hands on it, they once again tweaked the letterform, adding slight weight changes to correct optical illusions.

Drawing the I

The I has gone through many changes, and slab serif designs are the closest to its original inception. Most people are more familiar with the standard simplified design of one single stroke. I often use Lubalin Graph as an example of slab serif designs, because of its exaggerated serifs. The representation of an arm and hand has been distilled out of our present day I, which is the fourth most commonly used letter in the English language according to Oxford.

Drawing an I is almost self explanatory, you just use your common stem's width, and use the common serif if designing a serif face. Blackletter and calligraphy on the other hand offer a little more creativity. Some common blackletter typefaces contain an I that terminates with a tail that sweeps to the left, or a flourish on the top that starts on the left. A slab serif will have two thick horizontal bars capping off both the top and bottom of the stem.

Slab Serif

vertical stem

- Use your common stem.
- If designing a serif face, use your common serif.

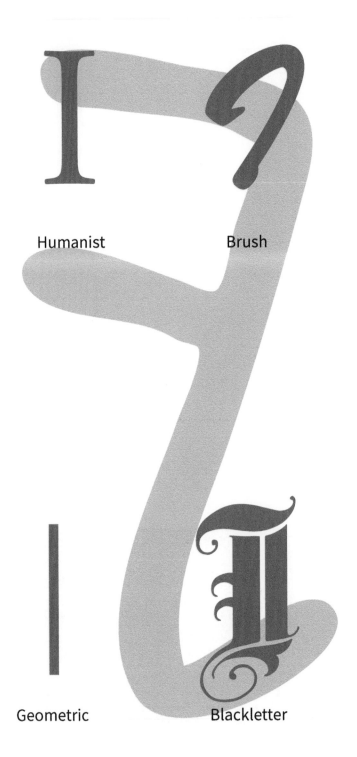

Humanist

Brush

Geometric

Blackletter

The lowercase i was first inked dotless, as a single stroke smaller than the capital. In later forms, the i had the dot added which carried through to our modern day designs.

J

J J J

ROMAN   FRENCH   ENGLISH

J

The J is represented by a sound created by forcing air between the tongue and the roof of the mouth. The J lacks the rich heritage, but it is used in many modern words like jazz, jive and jeep to name a few.

Unlike most of our letters, the J is a Western European invention. The Romans had no J sound in their language, but their I was the starting point for our present day J. The Romans grew more dominant throughout Europe, their alphabet spread with their conquests. Northwestern Europe used the the Roman alphabet, but they also developed a few of their own sounds, both the English and French developed a J sound. Their scribes started adding an empennage that angled to the left to differentiate their new letter from the existing Roman I.

Drawing the J

The J was a late addition to our alphabet, and its usage brings it to second from the last, just above the Q. As mentioned, it is based on the I and shares quite a bit until you get to the lower half of the letter. Many Germanic languages treat the J like we treat the Y.

Drawing the J is a little more complex than its predecessor the I. It too uses the common vertical stem, but it has its lower bowl. This bowl, like other curved letters, dips a bit below the baseline, to visually correct for the curvature. In traditional typefaces the bowl has stress, or weight variation at the lowest point of the curve.

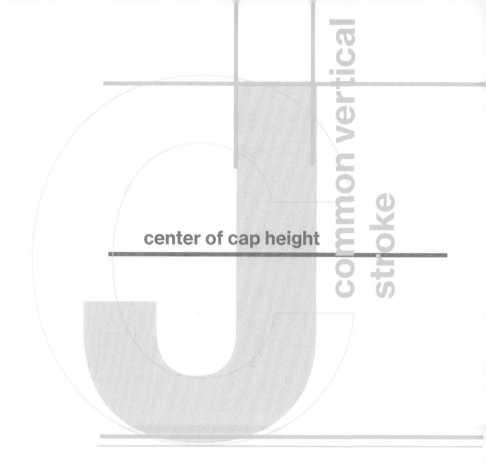

center of cap height

- The lower bowl floats down slightly like the C
- Let the C's curvature inspire the J's.
- Use the common vertical stem.
- Add stress to the lowest point of the curvature.

Humanist

Brush

Geometric

Blackletter

Like its capital counterpart, the j was a later additional, showing up in popular French designs on the 1600s dotted like the lowercase I. Modern day designs have widened the curved stroke on the bottom, creating a hook shape.

K

SEMITIC

EARLY PHOENICIAN   PHOENICIAN   EARLY GREEK

LATER ROMAN

K

Palm Reader

The sound representing a K is a forceful and sharp burst of air from the back of the throat. It is one of our more unique letterforms, it has a variety of shapes created by both postive and negative space. The slice of negative space on the right-hand side requires special attention be paid to kerning against the following glyph.

The K is a representation of something Fortune Tellers have always used for divining our futures, life lines. its roots go back to ancient Egypt, and it is their pictogram for the human hand. The early Semitic character looked similar to a U with two vertical strokes set in the middle. The Phoenicians named the letter Kaph, and their version mimicked the lifelines in the palm of the hand. Think of the symbology, the hands represent much, from the work of a carpenter, a loving touch and so much more.

When the Greeks got their turn they renamed it Kappa and over time, rotated the letter leftward, birthing the design only one step away from the present iteration. The Etruscans kept the Greek version intact, but the Romans flipped the letter horizontally to create the present-day version.

Drawing the K

The K, in my opinion, is one of the more difficult letters to draw, because there are many considerations to make during the design process. Some typeface designs have the lower leg begin on the upward stroke, while others, like Futura, have the upper and lower strokes meet the vertical stem at an angle similar to a rotated V.

Another detail to be considered is the space between the two angled legs. The negative space on the lower section (the area between the stem and diagonal stroke) is typically more than the negative space on the upper part of the letter. Otherwise, the K would be top heavy and awkward.

If you were to take a vertical rule and place it on the upper right-most corner, you would see the the lower diagonal stroke extends a hair beyond the top's. This visually corrects the letterform, so it doesn't appear to be tipping over. The weight of the angled strokes are lighter than the common vertical stem. This is a carryover from a pen and nib. Many designs also taper the two angled strokes at the point of convergence to visually lighten up the heavy look of the nexus of three strokes.

common vertical stroke

center of cap height

- The lower diagonal stroke extends beyond the top. Notice all of the tapering that occurs at the intersection of the three strokes.
- Use the common vertical stem.
- Adjust the negative space on the top and the bottom so they're not quite equal, the top being smaller.
- Taper the angled strokes to lighten up the point of convergence.
- Have the lower diagonal stroke extend a hair beyond the upper.

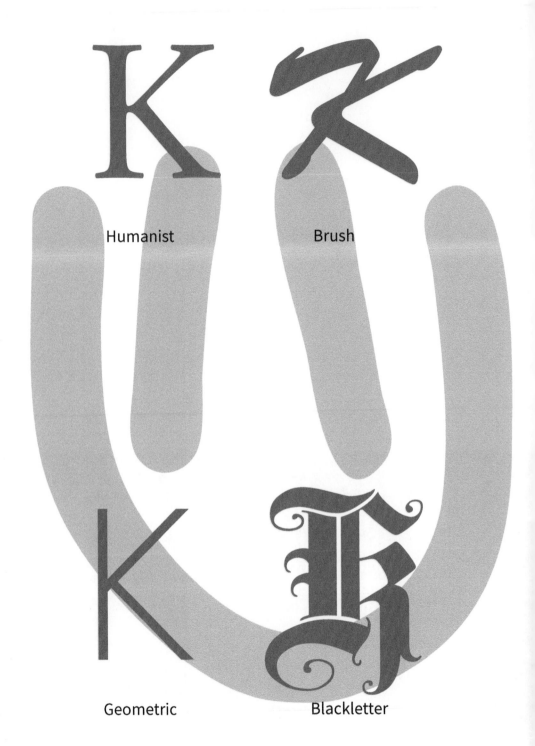

Humanist

Brush

Geometric

Blackletter

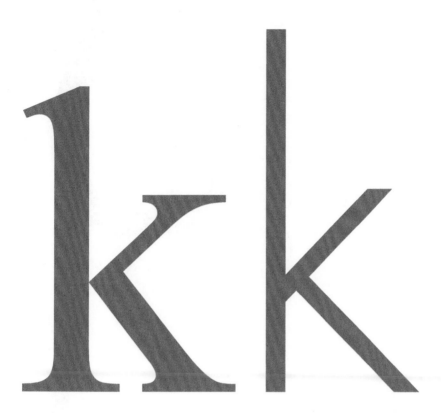

The lowercase k was a modified K created by handwriting in the mid-800s, the left vertical stroke kept its height, but the two diagonal strokes were reduced in size to match the other lowercase characters' height.

L

SEMITIC

PHOENICIAN

GREEK & EARLY ROMAN

LATER ROMAN

L
Goaded Along

We've all heard the phrase, "goad along" but little did we know that the goad, or something similar to a shepherd's staff, would be the inspiration for a letterform. The sound representing the L is created by forcing air between the tongue and roof of the mouth while seperating the two.

The L can trace its roots to Egypt, and the ancient Semites. Its Phoenician name is Lamed which translates into goad, and a goad is a cane-like tool used to herd Alephs, or oxen (refresh your memory in the chapter covering A). The ox must have been very important in the ancient world to inspire two letterforms.

The early Lamed looked similar to a J, the Phoenicians flipped it and made it more angular, like a check mark. The Greeks named it Lamda and yet again, flipped it. The Etruscans and the early Romans imitated the Greek's Lambda, but the Romans eventually flipped the letter again, and straightened up the angle to create the modern L.

Drawing the L

The L is another simple letter to design, and its history as a herding stick is rather ironic. The letterform has the ability to readily move your eye from the left to the right. The generous amount of negative space on the upper right can make it tough to kern with other letters, but with some special attention these issues can be resolved.

When drawing the L (unless you're creating a mono-weight design), use your typical vertical stem and horizontal stroke.

center of cap height

- Use the common vertical stem and horizontal stroke.
- The relationship to the E, the character is slightly narrower.

Humanist

Brush

Geometric

Blackletter

The lowercase l drew its inspiration from Latin handwriting. In this handwriting the foot of the uppercase L was greatly reduced. This simplification process carried on to the humanist designs which are still present today.

M

ᛗ
SEMITIC

ᛯ ᛘ ᛘ

EARLY PHOENICIAN   PHOENICIAN   GREEK

ᛉᛘ ᛘᛘ

EARLY ROMAN   ROMAN

M

The M is a very primitive sound, it is one of the first sounds an infant makes when calling its mother, or Mama. The lips and rear throat are utiliized to create this unique sound.

Most agree that the Mem is the early Semitic symbol for water, which composes 60–70% of the human body. The sharp angles were symbolic of waves, and more than likely, drawn sharply angled because they were scribed into clay. This basic substance, essential for life, has spawned wars, and aided in the growth of many historic port cities. The ancient Egyptians used the owl as the visual representation of the M sound. Many early Semitic drawings of the Mem were vertical rather than horizontal. The Phoenicians rotated it into a horizontal character.

The Greeks eventually clipped the right final stroke, and renamed it Meta. As the letterform moved through the Mediterranean, the Etruscans (as usual) maintained the Greek look and feel. The Romans, on the other hand, trimmed it down to the bare bones. removing any extraneous strokes.

Drawing the M

The M is a rather important letter in our alphabet, setting the tone for the width emdash. It represents one of human's most vital needs, water, so it makes sense that it has an important role in our alphabet. It is the 14th most commonly used letter in the English language. I highly recommend that you review a wide variety of Ms in many typefaces. You will note that there are many ways to treat it. Some designs have stems, while others add an angle to the left and right strokes.

Futura is an excellent example of angled strokes, and the left and right strokes meet at a shared point. If you look at Futura's M up close you will also note that the left and right strokes flare slightly as they move toward the baseline. This treatment is employed to visually lighten up the meeting of the four strokes.

Neue Haas Grotesk (used in the diagram) is a good example of a more vertical design. Note how the two top elements are wider than the vertical stem below. Also, notice how the two stems taper on the top or apexes, and the downward pointing center slice also tapers. So, you can see how you must make a number of adjustments to the stroke weights to keep the intersections from appearing too dense.

center of cap height

- The vertical strokes are narrower than the common vertical stem
- Note all of the tapering that occurs at the three inter-sections and the intersection in the center created by the two vertical strokes.
- Note the cut out ink trap highlighted on the top of the page.

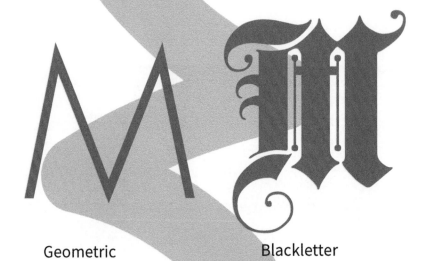

Humanist

Brush

Geometric

Blackletter

mm

Not much changed in the creation of the lowercase m.
In the mid-400s, the character's height was reduced and
the angles were replaced by softer, rounder shoulders,
or rounded strokes. This modification carried through to
modern day typeface design.

N

EARLY PHOENICIAN

EARLY GREEK   ETRUSCAN   EARLY ROMAN

ROMAN

N

Snake in the Grass or Fishy Business

One would think the letter S would be the early representation of the snake, but that would be incorrect. The credit goes to the N. N's roots were squiggled in the sands of Ancient Egypt as the glyph for the snake. Something slippery happened when it was transferred to the early Semites. They originally called it the Nahash, which also meant snake, but its appearance was short lived, and was changed to what the Phoenicians called the Nun, which symbolized fish. Maybe the fish was a little more important or palatable to a seafaring culture than a snake?

The Egyptian and early Semitic versions were rather gestural like a loose squiggle, then it became more angular when drawn by the Phoenician hand. The Greek's version was called a Nu, and it still was very similar to the Phoenician version. The Etruscans also made no changes. The Romans, once again did their typical horizontal flip, added a touch of geometry to the letterform creating our modern N.

Drawing the N

Knowing that the N is derived from a snake, it is also worth mentioning that it is the seventh most commonly used letter in the English language. It is used with a wide variety and combinations of other letters too, not just restricted to vowels. Designers should think of words like want, ring, sink, own and brawn when creating this letter.

The N's usage highlights its importance in proportion and relationship to other letters in a typeface. If you are designing a good starting point to determine the letter's width can be four-fifths of the M's width. This, of course, can be adjusted once you begin testing the letters against other members of your alphabet. Like the M, there are a few visual corrections that you should make to keep the stroke intersections from appearing thick and heavy.

Neue Haas Grotesk highlights (seen in diagram) this treatment, by tapering the pie-shaped angles where the vertical and diagonal strokes intersect.

center of cap height

- Make width equal to roughly four-fifths of the M.
- Taper the stroke on both sides, where the diagonal stroke intersects with both vertical strokes.
- Taper the intersection in the center created by the two vertical strokes.

N *N*

Humanist   Brush

N   N

Geometric   Blackletter

nn

The n, unlike the m, was a creation of the hands of medieval scribes in the 800s. This glyph, like others, was a simplification of the uppercase, reducing it to only two pen strokes. The angles were, like the m, replaced with a rounded shoulder.

O

SEMITIC

PHOENICIAN   GREEK   ROMAN

O

The Eyes Have It

The O is one of the more geometrically simple shapes in our alphabet, comprised of a complete circle. The sound we make to represent this character is created by rounding our mouths and forcing air through the backs of our throats.

The precursor to the O is the Egyptian hieroglyph for the eye. This primal shape was adopted by the early Semites and was named that sounded more like an A rather than O. They called it Ayin and the Phoenicians called it Eyn. Does that sound familiar? It should because it is the root of the letterform and, I am sure, our word for the human eye.

The eye has always been called the "window to the soul." Just think about how much emotion people show with their eyes, rage, sadness and joy quickly come to mind.

This common letter is one of the few that remained as-is throughout the course of history. The Greeks made a few minor tweaks to create their Omega and Omicron. The Omega was known as the Big O, and the Omicron was known as the little O. The Romans never created a variation.

Drawing the O

Eyes have often been called the windows to the soul, and knowing that our O is a representation of the human eye, it clarifies how important the O is to a typeface. Even though the O isn't one of our most commonly used vowels, it does set the stage for the design of other rounded letters.

Like other letters, the O still holds on to the weight variations created by a pen nib, with the thickest region of the stroke on both the right and left side of the character, with the thinnest being on the top and bottom.

If you're creating an O with a brush, special consideration should be given to the closure of the letterform, the brush typeface Mistral is a good example. Note how the stroke terminates by overlapping with the starting point. Another approach is completing the stroke by closing the circle, giving the impression of infinity.

vertical stem

center of cap height

- The stress of the character is on the top and bottom.
- Because the O is curved, the O should reach slightly below the baseline and above the cap height of other letters.

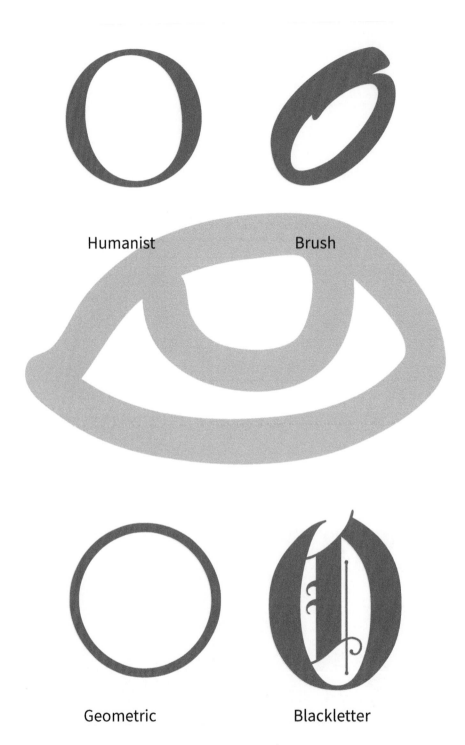

Humanist   Brush

Geometric   Blackletter

The lowercase o stems from Latin handwriting of the fifth century. It was reduced in height, and the stress of an ink pen gave the character the weight variation which we've become accustomed to in modern design.

P

PHOENICIAN

EARLY GREEK

EARLY ROMAN

ROMAN

P

Mouthing Off

The P started out as the Egyptian symbol for the mouth. You may find it quite apropos that the image for the mouth immediately follows the eye, perhaps it is just coincidental. The P is a primal sound that is akin to the M, think Mama and Papa. The early Semitic P had the look and feel of a V, the Phoenicians called it the Pe and drew it to resemble a primitive fish hook.

The early Greeks named it Pi, and that was their major overhaul. The Romans fine-tuned it, making it look more like a backward 7, later they created our present day P by drawing a semicircle closed by a lengthy vertical stroke.

The amount of negative space on the lower right gives it a unique challenge when kerning it against other letters. You will find you will always tighten the spacing so that the P visually connects to the next glyph.

Drawing the P

The P can be based on the common curves found in the B and R, but the lower horizontal bar will have to be visually adjusted and should reflect your commonly used horizontal stroke. You will want to taper the horizontal stoke at the intersection of the vertical stem.

In relatioship to the B, the central horizontal stroke typically meets the vertical stem lower than the B's and the stroke is the common thickness, unlike the B's, which has been thinned out to visually lighten up the stroke's intersection.

As an interesting aside, very possibly the person who invented the emoticon :p may not have known that our P is derived from the human mouth. The P is English's 13th most commonly used letter.

typical

typical

center of cap height

typical

- Let the curvature found in the B and R inspire the curve
- Use your common horizontal stroke to determine the lower horizontal stroke.

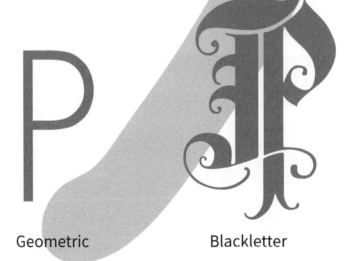

Humanist   Brush

Geometric   Blackletter

pp

The lowercase p was used in Latin manuscripts from the 600s, not much changed in the reduction process, other than turning the vertical stem into a descender.

Q

Q
Monkey Business or Knot?

The Q's sound comes from the same place that the K, C and G do, the back part of the throat. The Q has a similar sharp quality like the C and K. The back story on the Q is what I found very interesting.

The Q, is it monkey business or knot? This letter has an interesting origin. In its early inception, some say it may have been symbolic of a knot. Most agree that it eventually moved on to represent a qoph, which was the Phoenician word for monkey. The original glyph was a circle that had a vertical stroke running through its center and extended below the the circle.

The Greeks updated the name, calling it Qoppa and by cutting the stroke from the circle's center. The Romans yet again tidied up the glyph by treating it more like an O with a smaller tail.

Drawing the Q

The Q has always been one of my favorite letters, even though it is one of the least used letters in the English alphabet. Knowing that the Q is drawn from a rear view of a monkey, I now have insight into why I find the letter somewhat whimsical.

Obviously, the designer can use the O as the starting point for the design of this letter, but the tail of the Q is where this letter's spirit comes from. Some designs, such as Futura and Neue Haas Grotesk have an angled tail, using the common angled stroke weight. Many serif typefaces, such as Didot, have more of a calligraphic flourish for its tail.

Some brush designs, such as Mistral, use a single, highly stylized stroke that renders the Q with a singular stroke rather than two individual strokes.

center of cap height

vertical stem

- Like the O, the stress on the character is on the top and bottom.
- The letterform also sits slightly below and above of the cap height.
- Note the curved stroke slightly thins where the tail intersects (compared to the O).
- If your design has more of an angular stroke, you may taper the intersection of the tail and O shape. This visually thins out the positive space at the point of intersection.

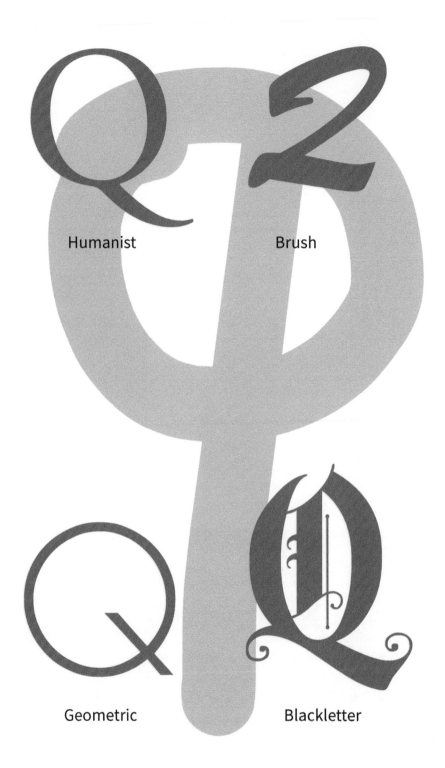

Humanist

Brush

Geometric

Blackletter

The lowercase q went through a number of redesigns. The first simplification can be seen in the Latin manuscripts of the seventh century. The tail of the q was replaced with a downward stroke or descender on the right side of the glyph. This was a time saving modification and carried through to today's modern typeface designs

R

EARLY SEMITIC

SEMITIC   EARLY GREEK   GREEK

ROMAN

R
Head and Shoulders

The Egyptian Ro was the symbol for the human head and shoulders, in a profile view. The glyph was rather obvious in its reference to the human head and shoulders, and is one of the earlier letter forms in the original alphabet. The Phoenicians decided to make simplifications in the letter-form, rename it Resh, then reduced it down to resemble our present day P. Being that the Phoenicians read from right to left, the simplified shape resembled a backward P.

The early Greeks didn't change the letter at all, except for renaming it Rho. The Etruscans adopted the letter as is, but once the letterform made its way to Rome, it had another major overhaul. The Romans wanted to differentiate the character from the P, so they added a right slanted leg. This addition gives the R a slight reference back to its original Egyptian counterpart.

There is plenty of visual activity happening in the R, so kerning it against other letters can be a little tricky, but it can make for a gorgeous letter pairing.

Drawing the R

The R's shape definitely resembles a human head. To me the resemblance is the strongest as a head in profile. The R is the third most commonly used letter in English, and its relationship to several other letters makes it somewhat simple to design. You can use the P and the B as starting points.

The P can be used to help you set up the size of the negative space, while the B can help you tweak the weights where the diagonal tail intersects with the upper half's counter.

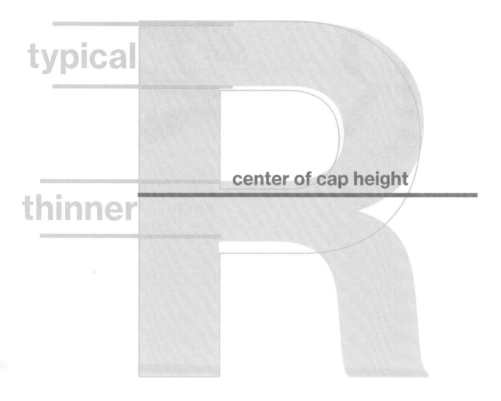

typical

thinner

center of cap height

- Comparing the R to the P shows that the hoizontal inter-section of the three strokes is floated down.
- Note how the two curved strokes taper dramatically where they meet in the central section of the glyph.
- Use the common curvature and stroke placement found in the P and B for continuity.

Humanist   Brush

Geometric   Blackletter

The lowercase r does not resemble its uppercase counter-part in any fashion, it is an extreme simplification of the R which was developed by medieval scribes as a time saver.

S

S

SEMITIC

W

Z

S

PHOENICIAN

GREEK

EARLY ROMAN

S

ROMAN

S

The S is a rather elegant glyph, with the serpentine play of positive and negative space. Our sound for it even resembles that of a snake. One would think that the ancient roots of the S would be a serpent, but not true, many believe that the early Semites drew the S to symbolize a bow, as in a bow and arrow. The early Semitic renderings look like the contour of a water buffalo's horns. The Phoenician called this character the Shin, which looks like our present day W. These too had a horned appeal. The Shin was their word for tooth. Perhaps this character was a pair of fangs?

When the Greeks got their hands on it they used it for their Sigma. They rotated the shape and deleted a stroke creating a shape that looked more like a modern day Z. Then the Romans added their typical panache to the letter by flipping it and eventually adding the modern curvature.

The S looks great against other letters, but like the R, it does require fine tuning when kerning against other curved letters such as O, U, C and B.

Drawing the S

As mentioned earlier, I was rather surprised to learn that the S is not based on a snake or even perhaps a simplification of a wave of water. Knowing that this letter is based on a bow, as in bow and arrow, we can think about tension. Tension is created when a pen makes such a wide variety of movements to draw the letter. The S is packed with a lot of movement, which creates tension between the S and the other letterforms it is set against.

In a traditional grotesque typeface, the stress on the letter is on the top and bottom. The right and left of the character is traditionally thicker than the top and bottom. Like all other rounded letters, the top and bottom extend slightly below the baseline and above the cap height. If you didn't make this correction, the rounded letters would look smaller when placed against a squared letter such as an E, L or F.

The central curve of the S is called the spine, which is one of the thicker parts of the glyph. This is a carryover from calligraphy and the way a pen is handled. The nib starts from the right, and as the nib draws the top, the weight gets lighter, and on the downward stroke, the weight once again gets thicker. On the final upward stroke on the bottom, it once again thins, then thickens up again.

Another visual correction worth pointing out is the lower curves are pushed a hair to the right and left. Refer to the following figure to see an example.

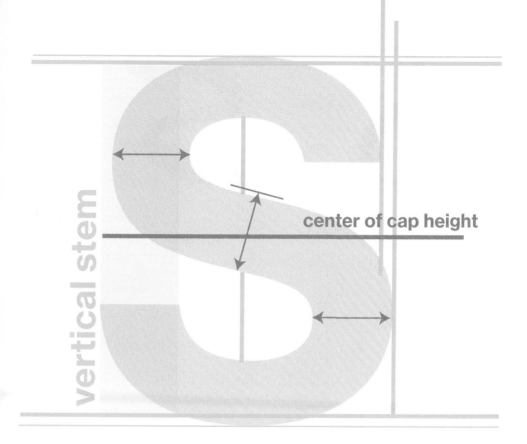

vertical stem

center of cap height

- The width of the lower half is noticably wider than the top.
- The distance between the central stroke is closer to the top than the bottom.
- The downward central stroke or spine's width is slightly thinner than the left and right side curves.
- Like other curved characters, the S is slightly taller than its squarer counterpart.
- Think of stress on a pen nib making a stroke when developing your weight variations in the letter form.

Humanist Brush

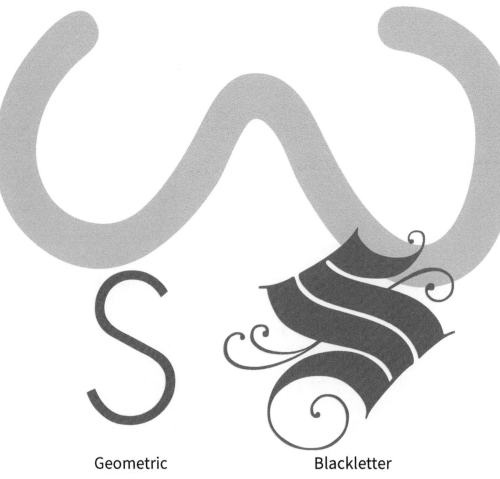

Geometric Blackletter

Ss

The creation of the lowercase s isn't as dramatic or extreme as the r, as you can see, it was just reduced in size. As David Sacks, the author of *Letter Perfect,* points out, the lowercase s was almost replaced by a glyph similar to the lowercase f.

T

PHOENICIAN

GREEK

ROMAN

T

The First Brand

We've all heard the phrase that possession is nine-tenths of the law, and perhaps this logic was elemental in the development of the letter T. The T is one of the more ancient glyphs in our alphabet. It was carved by the ancient Semites, and incorporated in the the early Phoenician alphabet. They named it Taw, which meant mark, and our forebears drew it like a simple plus sign. It is believed that they used the Taw to identify livestock and other possessions.

When the Greeks adopted this ancient letterform, they changed the name to Tau. They redesigned it by moving the horizontal stroke to the vertical's top. As per the norm, the Etruscans kept the Greek Tau intact, and passed the letter off to the Romans. In turn, they kept the letter as is.

The top heavy T creates its own kerning issue, namely the negative space around the lower section of the letterform. Lowercase letters will need to be tightened up against it so the T doesn't float off on its own. Plus, if the T is against a vertical letter such as an R, it will need some additional attention for the same reason.

Drawing the T

The T is the sixth commonly used letter in the English language. Like the P, if it is combined with an H it creates a second sound created by the tongue and upper mouth.

The T is an easy letter to draw, you start with your common vertical stem, and use your common horizontal stroke. The letter's width may be inspired by the N and/or the H.

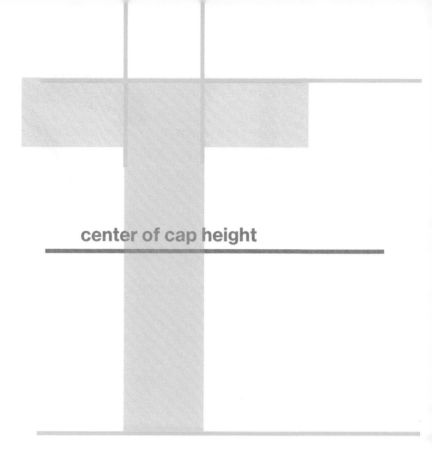

center of cap height

• Use your common vertical and horizontal strokes.

Humanist

Brush

Geometric

Blackletter

There was no lowercase version of the T until the Germanic form of calligraphy known as blackletter developed our current version in the 1200s. Up until then, the T stayed in its Roman form.

U

PHOENICIAN

ETRUSCAN

CARVED ROMAN

CLASSIC ROMAN

U
Another Peg

The U is an interesting vowel, it is commonly used as a prefix to indicate the opposite of the root word, such as unhappy, unhelpful and unattended. Perhaps it is because the U was a redraw of the F.

The foundation of the U is built upon the Waw or letter F. As you can imagine, the letter went through a major redesign over time. Remember that Waw was Phoenician for peg or nail. Perhaps our ancient relatives were busy building lots of wooden objects to hold nails and pegs in such esteem to spin off several letters.

The Greeks named their version Upsilon, and kept the peg or Y shape. The Etruscans in this case were the ones to make a major revamp. They cut the vertical stroke and created a shape akin to a V. I am sure you've seen carved Roman text where the U was replaced by a V, well this is why. The Romans adopted the V, and later added the curvature to the letter's bottom.

Drawing the U

The U and the F share a common ancestry, but that is where the similarities end. I like to use the width of the H as a starting point for the development of the U. Of course, as mentioned many times before, you'll want to tweak the width once you get the relationship set against other letters. The U is the 11th most commonly used letter, and it is used with a wide variety of other letters.

When designing a grotesque typeface, you will want to use your common vertical stroke on both the left and right sides. In the lower curvature, you should make the weight thin out.

In a more calligraphic or old style typeface, you should make your left stroke the common thick weight and the right side your standard thinner weight.

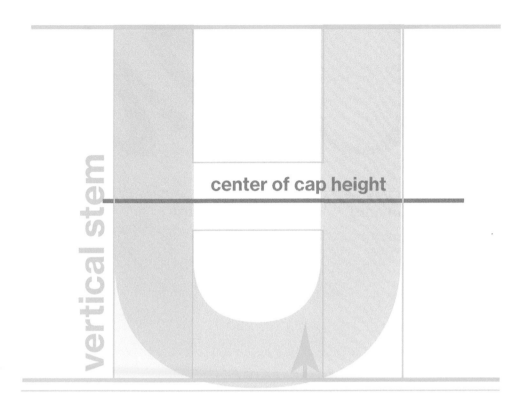

vertical stem

center of cap height

- The H can assist you in the width of your U.
- The lower curve floats down, but because the top is sqaure, you should maintain your cap height.
- Use your common curved stroke width for the bottom of the character, use stress similar to O's.
- The weight of the vertical strokes depends on the style of typeface you're designing.

U Humanist

 Brush

U Geometric

 Blackletter

The lowercase u made its debut in the seventh century. It was used in Latin manuscripts, and had a rounded bottom with a vertical stroke on the right side. This glyph stayed in this state until present day.

EARLY GREEK

V
From a Vortex

I've always viewed the sound of a V as a rather violent and abrupt sound created by the teeth and lower lip. It starts off many unpleasant words such as violence, vengeful and vertigo.

Like the other letters that bring up the rear, the V wasn't developed in Phoenicia or Egypt, but rather Rome. They kept the V after designing the U, not changing much along the lines. Originally the V was a carved U, but after text markings moved to paper and pen from chisel and stone, the U became what we know today.

The V doesn't have a glamorous background, but the letter definitely has visual drama, with bold strokes and stark angles. The V too also comes with kerning baggage, all of the negative space around the bottom points tends to make it float away from its neighboring letterforms: Negative kerning will have a positive effect.

Drawing the V

The V may seem like a pretty straightforward letterform, but there are several tweaks worth mentioning. The V is one of the lesser used letters in the English language, and according to Oxford, it ranks 22nd.

I like to base my uppercase V's width on the Y. You can use the Y's width as a starting point for the V, but as always, a little finessing may be required to create visual harmony. You may notice that the vertical strokes on many Vs are thinner than that of the Y's. This helps to keep the letter-form from becoming dense at the intersection, or crotch of the two angled strokes.

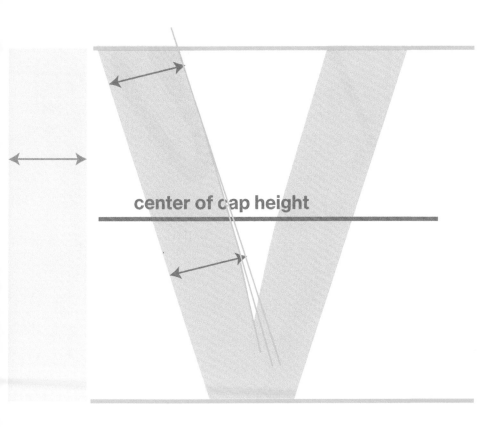

center of cap height

- Notice how the diagonal stroke begins with the same width as the common stem, but tapers several times on its way to the intersection of the two strokes, or crotch.
- If the design was a humanist or old style typeface, the left weight would be thicker than the right.
- Make your angled strokes thinner than the Y's.

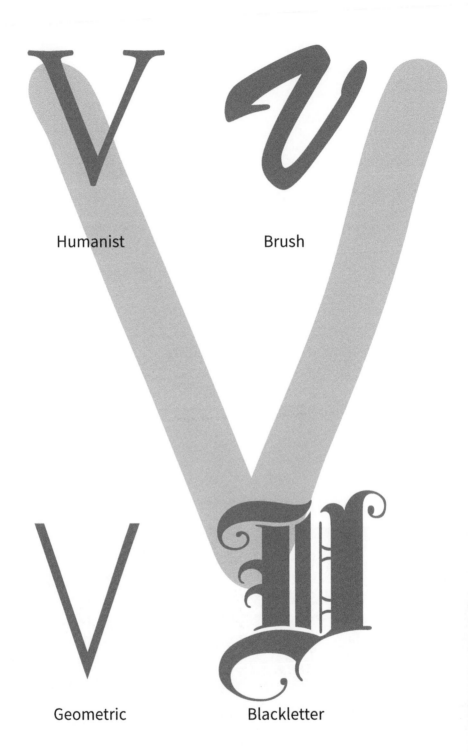

Humanist

Brush

Geometric

Blackletter

The lowercase v is obviously a reduced version of its up-perclass predecessor. There have been slight variations within typefaces, but nothing that changes the source characteristics of the glyph.

GERMAN AND ENGLISH

W

Two U's

Initially, I thought that perhaps the W originated from some horned mammal, like a bull or some other large grazing animal. But, no, its origins are much less glamorous. The roots of the W are similar to those of the J, both the Germans and English used two U's to indicate their W sounds. The German's W is much sharper than the English W, closer to the sound of our V. Initially, they used two U's (or Latin V's), which were drawn, and/or set very close to each other, eventually the two U's (or Latin V's) were merged into a single letterform.

This is one of the wider letters in our alphabet and has a multitude of angles and strokes. Like the V, it requires tweaking to make it visually connect with its neighboring letterform, especially if it is next to a rounded character.

Drawing the W

The W is an odd letter, in that it is a fusion of two repeating letterforms. Depending on the design, it will likely be one of the wider letters in your alphabet. According to Oxford, the W is the 20th most commonly used letter in our alphabet.

The W requires quite a bit of visual tweaking to keep all of the joints from becoming too dense. The letter, like the M, may need three ink traps and several stroke weights. Every sharp angle requires tapering of the strokes at each point of intersection.

You can use the same stroke weight used on the V to create your W, but you should reduce the two pie shapes on the left and right.

common vertical stroke

center of cap height

• The W has many optical corrections in the design, both left   and right strokes start out with the common width, but dramatically taper to visually lighten the stroke intersections. The interior strokes are thinner than the exterior strokes.
• Make your angled strokes thinner than the Y's.

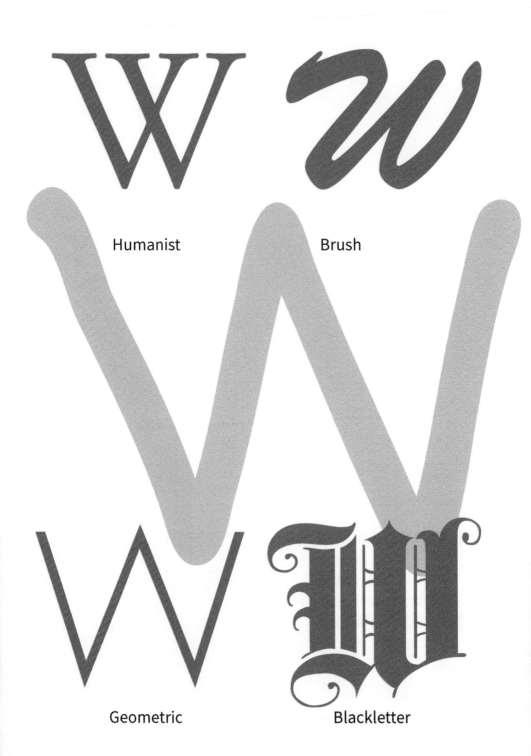

Humanist

Brush

Geometric

Blackletter

Due to the fact that the w is a late addition to our alphabet, I believe that is why there isn't any difference other than scale to the uppercase and lowercase versions of this letter.

X

X

Fishy Business

The Egyptians may have influenced the Phoenicians with the development of their glyph name Djed. The Djed symbolized strength in the form of a pillar. Most agree that the Phoenicians took the inspiration and developed the Samekh which represented a fish. There are differing opinions of whether it represented a living fish or rather a skeleton. I tend to think that it is a top view with gills, pectoral and ventral fins with an extended line indicating the tail fin.

As you can see in the illustrations, the Greeks simplified the letterform naming it Xi, removing the vertical stroke, but added it back again. It seems unclear as to whether the Greeks finalized the look of the letter by making the modern X or it if happened at some point between the Etruscans or Romans. Needless to say, the Romans bumped the letter up a notch by fine-tuning the geometry and stroke weight.

Drawing the X

The X's beauty is the X's symmetry. Though its roots are Piscean, its present day iteration has a reputation for such things as marking spots. The X's beauty is created by its negative space, which is almost equal to the importance of its positive space. The X is one of the lesser used letters in the English language, in fact it is in the lowest three in usage.

 If you take a close look at many X's, you will note that in many instances the strokes have minor adjustments where the two strokes intersect. At times, the strokes may have a slight taper. Also, the white pie shape or negative space on the top and bottom may cut into the intersection to visually lighten up the intersection. Another adjustment to make the letterform easier on the eye is to widen the width on the lower half of the character.

center of cap height

- As with the S, the negative space on the top of the X is smaller than the bottom, and the bottom half's width is slightly wider.
- Notice the amount of tapering implemented to visually lighten up the interior of the character. The strokes begin with the common width, but taper towards the center.

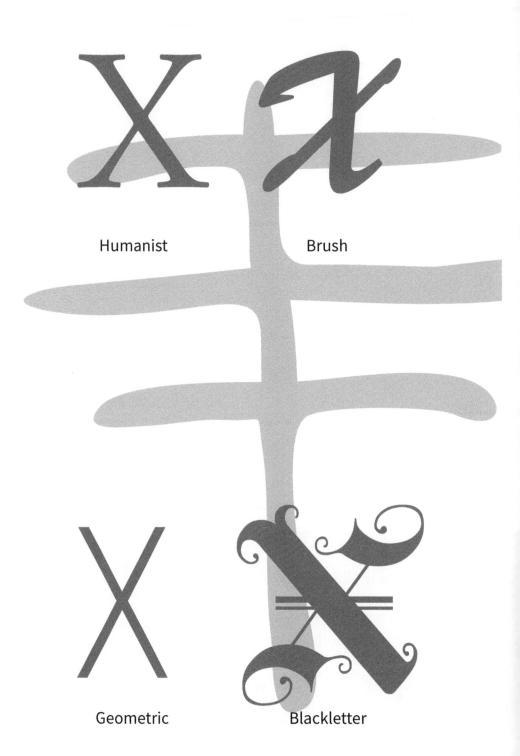

Humanist

Brush

Geometric

Blackletter

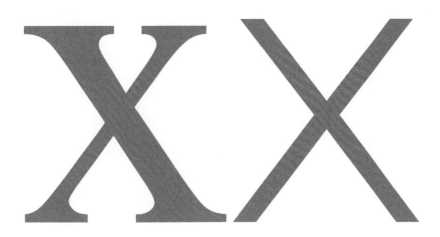

The lowercase x can be seen in Latin manuscripts from the seventh century. Like the C, M, U, P and V, there isn't much difference between the upper and lower cases. The X is made with two simple diagonal strokes that intersect in the visual center.

ROMANS

Y

When in Rome

The Y is another letter that the Romans developed, think of it as a late addition to their alphabet. It was based on the Greek vowel Upsilon. In English, Y has double duty as a consonant and a casual vowel. As with the last few letters in our alphabet, this letter doesn't have any reference to an animal or inanimate object.

Like the X, K and V, the Y can require some kerning finesse when placed against a rounded letter or for that matter a vertical one too. An abundance of negative space on the bottom of the character can make it appear as the Y is another word, standing solo. You may even tuck your lowercase letter slightly under the right side's diagonal stroke.

Drawing the Y

The Y may not have been one of the Phoenician's original characters, but its split purpose as a vowel and consonant makes it a wider used letter than many other late additions to our alphabet, and is 19th on Oxford's usage list.

I like to base my uppercase Y on the X, if you split the difference between the width of the X's top and bottom, it sets up a pleasant width for the Y. Of course, you should use your common vertical stroke for the lower part of the Y, and as always, you should taper the angled strokes as they intersect.

You can also use the lowest point on the X where the two lower legs meet to set up the height for the Y's vertical stroke.

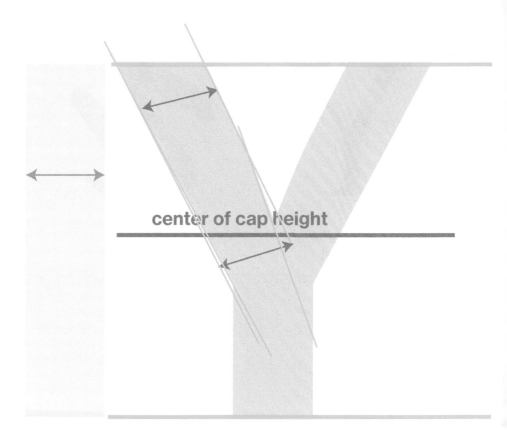

center of cap height

- The intersection of the Y is further down the character than the X, but the tapering is quite similar.
- The vertical stroke is your common stem weight.

Humanist

Brush

Geometric

Blackletter

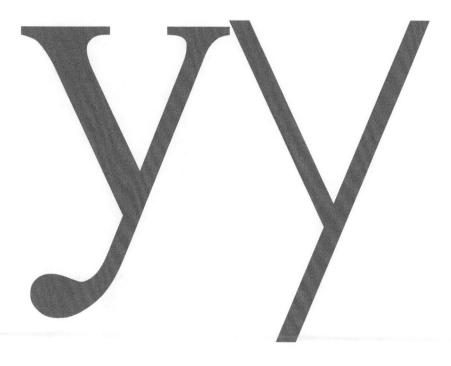

The lowercase y was drawn by Latin scribes in the seventh century. The object was simplification, having two simple pen movements rather than three.

Z

SEMITIC

PHOENICIAN

EARLY GREEK

GREEK

ROMAN

Z

Now last but not least, we have the Z, which started off in early Phoenicia as Zaylin. It more than likely represented a weapon. To me it represents a dagger, but as David Sacks, author of *Letter Perfect,* posits, perhaps an axe.

The Z went through some noticeable updates over time. The early Semitic and Phoenician Zayin looked a little like a telephone pole, comprised of one long vertical stroke with two cross-strokes on the top of the glyph. The Phoenicians eventually moved the lower horizontal stroke to the bottom creating a letter similar to an uppercase I. The Greeks adopted the later Zayin and renamed it Zeta. They eventually slanted the vertical stroke to the right to create the modern Z. The Romans added the Zeta, unchanged, to complete their alphabet.

Drawing the Z

The Z's shape is similar to the N, but the commonality ends there. The Z may be the last letter in the alphabet, but it isn't the last in usage frequency, there it sits toward the end, as the 24th most commonly used letters. Whether the Z started off as a dagger or axe, its foundation is definitely utilitarian.

It is one of the simpler letters to draw, you use your common horizontal weight on both the top and bottom. You will also develop a custom width for the diagonal stroke.

The Z is typically slightly narrower than the N, and you should of course adjust your widths by testing against other letterforms. This keeps your typeface's visual rhythm visually appealing. Where the diagonal stroke meets the two horizontal strokes, you should taper all intersecting lines to visually lighten up the intersections.

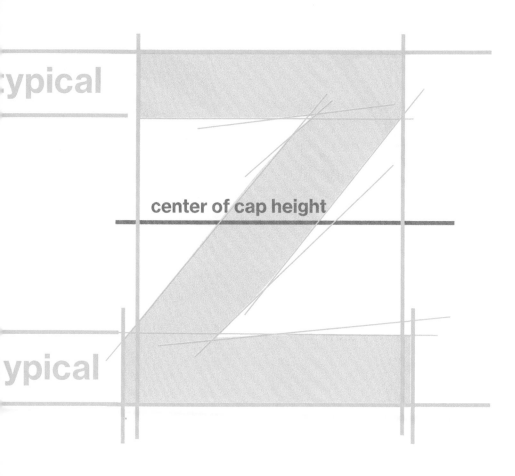

typical

center of cap height

typical

- The Z has a fair amount of tweaking, considering it is such a simple and angualr shape, but as the diagram shows, every intersection has several visual corrections, all tapering at the point of convergence.
- Note that the bottom of the character is wider than the top, as with the S, X, and B.

Humanist

Brush

Geometric

Blackletter

The lowercase z is a smaller version of the capital Z, with no design changes or alterations.

Letter Frequency

Many European languages have common letter combinations that create unique challenges, and kerning is the solution to these challenges. Some examples include: Dutch's OO, English's TH and CH. These letter combinations create visual rhythms that keep the eye moving through a page or a dynamic motion in a logo design. Kerning plus the negative space of your design will aid in readability.

Some of the most common two-letter combinations or bigrams include: TH, ER, ON and AN. There are also a few common repeating letterforms that occur in the English language, think of SS, TT and FF.

ETAOIN SHRDLU may remind you of Greeked text or the place-holding Lorem Ipsum, but it is a handy little phrase that contains some of the most commonly used letters in English.

Many of these character combinations have kerning challenges, and the following diagrams will highlight them.

TH, ER, ON, AN

Kerning pairs are sets of glyphs that need special attention by the designer to their relationships. A good example is an L and a U. The L's negative space created by the bottom horizontal stroke needs to be tightened up to close the negative space created by the U's curve.If you wish to go further down the rabbit hole of type design, you will need to kern your letterforms. I have always liked Kern King, which is a few paragraphs of copy that contains many of the kerning pairs that will turn your font into eye candy.

L & U

Kern King can be found at: http://logofontandlettering. com/kernking.html

The Concise Oxford Dictionary (11th edition revised, 2004) published the following table showing the most commonly used letters in descending order:

E	11.1607%	56.88
A	8.4966%	43.31
R	7.5809%	38.64
I	7.5448%	38.45
O	7.1635%	36.51
T	6.9509%	35.43
N	6.6544%	33.92
S	5.7351%	29.23
L	5.4893%	27.98
C	4.5388%	23.13
U	3.6308%	18.51
D	3.3844%	17.25
P	3.1671%	16.14
M	3.0129%	15.36
H	3.0034%	15.31
G	2.4705%	12.59
B	2.0720%	10.56
F	1.8121%	9.24
Y	1.7779%	9.06
W	1.2899%	6.57
K	1.1016%	5.61
V	1.0074%	5.13

X	0.2902%	1.48
Z	0.2722%	1.39
J	0.1965%	1.00
Q	0.1962%	(1)

Further information can be found at https://en.oxforddictionaries.com/explore/which-letters-are-used-most.

Numerals

Our modern Hindu-Arabic numerals evolved out of self-awareness, the notion that you are numero uno, and everyone else is secondary. We have two hands and feet, each with five digits. so it is natural that special attention was paid to the first set of 10 digits. Our ancestors found themselves needing a method of accounting for both ownership, dating and mercantile purposes.

The Romans and Greeks took a while to adopt the Hindu-Arabic numerals, as you may remember (take note of movie credits to refresh your memory), the Romans used Roman numerals while the ancient Greeks used a scoring system utilizing some vertical strokes. The Romans used a single stroke for the number one, adding an additional stroke for two through three. Five was represented by a V, 10 by X, L was 50, C was 100, D was 500, and M was 1000.

As James Allenson Picton, author *The Origin and History of the Numerals*, cites, two has a tie to the Latin du-o or the pronoun for you. So, I am one and you are two. Three has its roots in Sanscrit, tri, which is to exceed. Many words have their roots with the numeral three like trespass and troupe. Picton also states that four started off as "Chattri" Eka-cha-tri, which meant one and three. This was eventually reduced to chatur. Latin changed the spelling to quatuar.

Five was representative of our hands and toes. The Sanskrit root of five is an outstretched hand.

The Sanskrit origins of six, shash, was simply the doubling of three.

Seven is the Sanskrit saptan.

Eight's Sanskrit numeral was Ashtau, which is understood to represent a duplicated four. The Sanskrit for nine was Navan which represents the idea of new.

Sanskrit 10, das'an, was changed to decem in the Latin language.

Drawing the 1

Use your common vertical stroke

vertical stem

Drawing the 2

Use your common horizontal stroke on the bottom of the numeral, let your B, P and R inspire the curvature on the upper right. I also let the S assist in drawing the curved diagonal down stroke. Where the downward stroke meets the horizontal stroke on the bottom, both elements should taper as they meet.

Drawing the 3

Use your B to assist in developing your curves. The width of the glyph's upper half should be slightly narrower than the lower half.

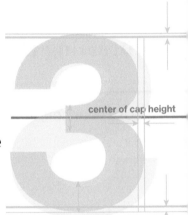

center of cap height

Drawing the 4

Use your common vertical and horizontal strokes, but your angled stroke should be thinner than the two. This third thickness is a holdover of an angled calligraphy pen. You should also taper the diagonal and horizontal strokes where all angles meet to avoid a visually dense glyph.

Drawing the 5

I commonly use the S to help inspire my fives. Use your common horizontal stroke at the top, and vertical stroke on the upper left, but let the curve on the lower right be inspired by your S. Some common typefaces add additional width to the bottom of the glyph, making a thinner curved stroke than a capital S, C or G.

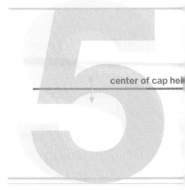

Drawing the 6

The six is an interesting glyph. You can get the left side's curve from the C, but you will want to pay close attention to the form's stress on the bottom curve and where the center curve turns back into the character.

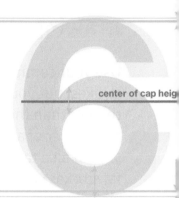

center of cap heig

Drawing the 7

Use your common horizontal stroke on the top, and let the diagonal stroke be inspired by your 4. The diagonal stroke should be a little narrower at the top, and widen on the down stroke.

174

Drawing the 8

The eight requires some additional consideration, unlike other glyphs, the eight has the intersection of two curved strokes. The intersection will require some visual adjustments to keep the region from becoming visually heavy.

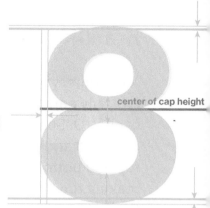

center of cap height

Drawing the 9

Many popular typefaces use a flipped 6 for their 9, you may want to test your 9 against other letters and numbers to see if you need any adjustments.

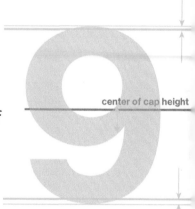

center of cap height

The 9 usually is a rotated 6 and like other rounded letters, the digit's top and bottom extend beyond the squared ones.
Like the 5, 3 and 6, the stroke weight at the intersection of the two curves is thinner than the top and bottom's weight.

Drawing the 0

The 0 differs from the O, the glyph is typically narrower than the capitol O. Some common designs even add additional stress to the top and bottom of the character, making the stroke thinner than the O. As with other rounded glyphs, the 0 is slightly taller than its flatter counterparts.

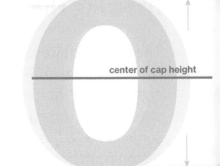

center of cap height

Designskolen Kolding

I was invited to teach a type design workshop at Denmark's Designskolen Kolding and couldn't resist the concept of including some of the students' work and highlighting their design process. In addition to teaching a week-long course I also lectured, and my lecture included an overview of the origins of our modern alphabet. I wanted to see how this knowledge affected the student's design process.

The project was to design a typeface using either found imagery or their own photography. I wanted them to explore the concept of using a pictogram to represent a letterform rather than using traditional strokes. One student explored type design by cutting up an existing typeface, and using the stems and pieces to create his own alphabet. The results were something akin to "The Island of Dr. Moreau." The letterforms ended up having a visual rhythm, some stroke weights were reversed which gave headlines an abstract feel.

Another student photographed his dog, constructing a typeface using nostrils, fangs, teeth and ears. This typeface reminded me of of cave paintings, obviously the color added a modern twist. Once the student put the typeface into use by setting a headline in the typeface creating a specimen, the face ended up having a very primitive look.

One young student designed a typeface by arranging his socks, creating one of the more whimsical projects out of the group. My initial thought was that it would be a great font for a mother to notify her son that he must clean up his room.

A young woman decided to push the envelope and do brush work, on a rather large scale, for each letter about 5 inches in height. The majority of her letters had unexpected points of stress in each letter, the thicker part of the stroke was in an unusual place. This design method gave her alphabet a Middle Eastern feel. Each letterform also had a ribbon-like quality, due to the high contrast in the stroke weight.

Following is the work and descriptions from a few students who wanted to participate in this publication.

Oskar Risbjerg Martinussen

The project

My font is called "DOG", simply because it is made by close-up pictures of my dog. My working process mainly consists of: command c and command v. As the picture shows (see page 183) I simply marked out an area, copied it and pasted it into another document. Then I started creating letters and slowly building up the font. I reused a lot of the same shapes like you do when you create a normal font, for example the O, U, D, B and C are all made up from the E, which consists of the nose. When putting together the font, I wanted to keep the 3D look from the pictures, so that they could stand out on the final poster. This was needed because without it, the textured surface and many different colours would just disappear.

About me

My name is Oskar and I am studying communication design at Designskolen Kolding in Denmark. My main focus in my education lies on interaction design, so I concentrate most of my time focusing on the user. That is where I feel I can really make a difference by noticing the detail that creates the idea and foundation of the design. When all that is said, your crafts are just as important. You have to able to speak the language of a graphic designer, photographer or other craftsmen, if you ever want to have proper collaboration. Great designs are made in groups.

Oskar can be contacted via email at osma1303@dskd.dk

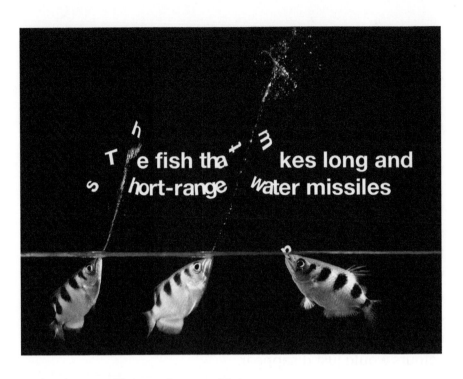

Oskar's type illustration project

"THE CONCEPT OF GLOBAL WARMING WAS CREATED BY AND FOR THE CHINESE..."

- DONALD TRUMP

ABCDEFGHIJKLMNOPQRSTUVWXYZÆØÅ

Oskar's dog-inspired typeface

Hans August Kirkemann Friis

About the font

Reinkated is a wordplay on reincarnated and ink. I thought that described the essence of the font pretty well, as it was created by practically "killing" the font Georgia, cutting it to pieces and reincarnating it by putting back the bits (the ink that it consists of) in new ways. For instance, the leg of the uppercase R is taken from the tail of the Q and vice versa. While the X consists of the arms and legs from a lowercase and an uppercase K tilted clockwise and counterclockwise, respectively. Note: No letters were harmed during the making of this font.

About me

I'm a graphic and interactive designer with my main focus on user experience and interface design. I think beauty is found where contrasts meet. Two of the things that mean the most to me are digital user interfaces and wild nature. That might seem paradoxical, but we are part of nature, and it's my belief that we should remember that in everything we do.

Hans can be contacted via email at hans.august@gmail.com or connect with him on linked in by searching Hans August Kirkemann Friis.

Rein- kated

The wizard quickly jinxed the vaporising gnomes, before shouting:

"PACK MY BOX WITH FIVE DOZEN LIQU- OR JUGS"

Hans' hand-drawn type illustration

INTERVIEWS

Typography now has many disciplines, as in the medical industry, and over the years designers have created areas of expertise. Rather than podiatrists, dermatologists and ENTs, the applied arts have way-finding specialists, type designers and UI professionals. I wanted this book to have a chapter featuring discussions with designers from some specialized disciplines.

I have interviewed several of my colleagues to get insight into their design process. We have a motion graphics designer, type and logo designer and a UI specialist. Each designer has also supplied work samples that highlight their personal aesthetic and individual approach to problem solving.

Jürgen Weltin

Jürgen Weltin runs the independent type design studio Type Matters, located south of Munich. Leaving his roots at Lake of Constance to study graphic design and doing early design works in publishing houses, design studios and industrial design firms, he soon discovered a passion for type design. He began creating his first typefaces in the 1990s, and worked as a type designer at The Foundry in London to broaden his skills. He received a D&AD award for a commissioned telephone book typeface for the Yellow Pages directory. His first typeface family Finnegan® was licensed into the Linotype typeface library in 1997 and received a Certificate of Excellence in Type Design at bukva:raz! (first type design competition of ATypI). These early awards encouraged him to start his own design studio in 2001 doing graphic and typographic design works, logotypes, typographic consultancy and lecturing typography regularly at design schools. And, most of all, to design type independently, doing custom type work for various clients, optimizing corporate fonts and extending their language support. His own designs also include the display, stencil-like typeface Balega®, the 33 styles of the Agilita® sans serif typeface family, Mantika Informal®, an easy to read typeface with reading beginners in mind, brought into form through a slightly inclined italic to bridge the gap between a handwriting script and a first reading typeface. Then came Mantika Sans® which was designed to be clearly legible in small sizes. It received an award at Granshan International Eastern Type Design Competition in 2010 for its Greek alphabet. This was followed up by an old-style design called Mantika Book®. The Mantika type system will be completed by another style called Mantika News®. His latest typeface design is an innovative, bilingual Hebrew-Latin alphabet called Julius Roman whose Hebrew letters are based on the Hebrew Cursive script.

www.typematters.de
twitter.com/type_matters
weltin@typematters.de

When you design letters for a logo which will only be set against letters in the company's name, do you approach them in the same way you do for a complete typeface?

[JW] No, normally not. Why not? Because a logo is a static sign, whereas letters for a typeface always need to function having new and different neighbors next to them. Hence reading a logo(type) is different from reading a line of text. There might be the issue of repeating letter shapes in a company's name which could look too sterile in a display typeface. So, the logotype might look more coherent when repeating letters are designed with slight differences (see Challenge logotype on page 194). But even in a neutral typeface this issue can't be neglected. In the logotype for ShellChemicals, for example, which is based on Futura caps, the letters H, E and L have all different widths because the surrounding white space before and after those letters is significantly different (see ShellChemicals logotype on page 196). This is the same with the old Price-WaterhouseCoopers logo: none of the repeating letters are exactly the same (see PriceWaterhouseCoopers logotype on page 194). Some companies want their logotype to be set in their corporate typeface. But not every text typeface is ideal for display use and quite often logos also need to function in very small sizes. In such cases it is better to design new letters just for the logotype. It might be necessary to increase the distance between letters or to make the letters bolder to work well in small sizes (some companies have different logo designs for different sizes!). For this company, the logotype was drawn different from its corporate typeface ›Rotis‹.

See additional corporate logo designs by Jurgen Weltin on pages 194, 195 and 196.

What is the first letter you design to set the visual tone for the entire typeface?

[JW] Out of habit I start with the small letter ›n‹ in most cases because to me the visual tone begins on how the vertical stem interacts with the horizontal part of the letter and how this flows down again into the second vertical. Next is the letter ›b‹ where the horizontal flows into the round shape. Yet sometimes, I try to put these tones first into the more complex letter ›a‹.

Now that logos are used in web animations, corporate videos and app launch screens, do you take these into consideration while designing the letterforms?

[JW] Not at first thought. The same principles for the use of logos in different printing conditions or applied to different materials (minted, for example) also apply to screen use. A logo needs to appear perfect on the clip of a pen as well as on a mobile app. If I know that a logo will have to hold his own in a multitude of uses, I take these into consideration from the outset.

What tools do you use to develop both your typefaces and logos? Do you create your letterforms old school, with pens and pencils, or do you start working on a computer?

[JW] Both. It always depends on the projects and the ideas I have in mind for them. Sometimes I need pen and paper, sometimes I need a drawing software to start with. Once you're accustomed to sketch on a computer you'll start there immediately, which I have done often with my latest letterforms.

One thing I've noticed in your logo work is that you avoid trends and you create corporate identities that don't date themselves within a few years. How do you allow current design trends to influence you, but not override your aesthetic?

[**JW**] Well first, I try to give my clients something of value. In the case of an identity, to me, it doesn't appear very trustworthy to change your image every couple of years—unless you are a company or a service provider who needs to demonstrate that you live with and at the cutting edge. I do observe current design trends, but I try to filter out what is only a nine days' wonder and what is trying to jump on a popular train. If you don't want to do what everybody else does (where would be the differentiation?) and you want to be creative you have to make your own experiments. There is always talk about the rising individualization of our society. Yet I can't see it. People all behave the same, take all the same selfies, consume all the same products, wear all the same current fashion. If you find your own point of view there is less risk that trends override your behavior and your powers of perception when you do design work.

Is there any time period or design movement that inspires you?

[**JW**] Not specifically. I do like the early graphic design works when it wasn't called as such and when there was no education for it yet, but when artists entered the field of applied graphic art. Or the design works of the 1960s and 1970s when it was all still manually drafted and produced. On the other hand, I found it fascinating when all this shifted to be done with the help of computers and the use of computers enabled new aesthetic voices. I am inspired when I can sense some human craftsmanship in any kind of design.

You once mentioned you had a teacher name Volker Lehmann, who was inspirational to you. Can you please discuss his techniques and expound on his teaching techniques, touching on how his approach defined your design approach and your teaching style?

[JW] He was the first who taught me to look very closely at drawings and paintings and he explained the techniques to me that were necessary to create them. He also showed me some of the techniques and taught me how to use them. I was amazed what you could do with a set of sharpened pencils—the ones with the highest degree of hardness were my favorite ones. We had a very small printing shop at school where he printed my etchings and mezzotint plates. We spent hours in there after school because I've done lots of plates—all at the age between 17 and 21. To learn all the aspects that make a good print was a good experience. Yet his own graphic work was outstanding—I've never seen such meticulous lithographs. His drawings are so fine, you can't see a line. In any case, this early ›school of seeing‹ taught me to look at things differently and someday woke my interest in graphic design. Later on I found typography and typedesign very attractive. It was maybe this early consciousness for details that lead me there. To have an eye for detail (without neglecting the whole scope of a design work) is the one thing I try to teach my students.

Andersen Consulting

CHALLENGE !

PRICEWATERHOUSECOOPERS

Schwarzwald Sprudel

RSV Solidarität
Pullach

SHELLCHEMICALS

créono

1964 – 2014
50 Jahre Partnerschaft
Pauillac – Pullach

Leon A. Tinker

Leon A. Tinker has been working in design, advertising, marketing and promotions since 1990. His love for learning, teaching and inquisitive nature has spawned a career that has spanned over 20 years. Asking the right questions and being vested in the client's interests have resulted in award-winning results.

He's collaborated with entertainment brands, broadcast and cable networks with thoughtful relevant insight through strategy/image, brand development, integrated marketing, brand evolution, launch campaigns and overall brand cohesion.

An open mind. Passionate. Motivator. Fun.
Leon enjoys the experience of living.

When you animate words, do you prefer to treat each letter individually or treat the entire word as a unit?

[LT] Each problem has it's own solution.
It truly depends.It's usually easier to work backward.
The final resolve of the animation is the destination.
What's the most interesting way to get there.
I tend to look at the the sum of its parts that make up the

whole. So the answer to your question I would say....
I prefer to treat each letter individually.

What is your favorite typeface to use for animation? When you select a typeface for an animated project, do you aim for the ease of readability or more of an impactful approach?

[LT]Typography is such a skilled art and luckily designers have so many to choose to help illustrate and convey messaging.I can't say that I have a favorite typeface to animate.

The animation direction is informed/inspired on the assignment, the category, product, subject, the brand and the target. The objective is to reveal the logo or title in the most interesting way in time and space.

Readability is extremely important. But sometimes it may take a back seat depending on the narrative. The goal is to be impactful. Animation is a choreography. A dance that takes place between forms. Everything has a role and a responsibility, equally important. I think that readability and being impactful work hand in hand.

If your final execution has both, and the recipient connects from it being memorable and providing a meaningful experience, then mission accomplished.

Do you prefer serif or sans serif when animating type?

[LT] I don't have a preference. Font selection is dependent on creative license. Because we are in the business of service and we collaborate with our clients, it's the animator's responsibility to bring the typography to life with intention and purpose.

Do you ever draw your own typography, or do you stick to fonts that you license?

[LT]It truly depends on the assignment and the project. I think the natural approach is to start with a licensed font. Stick with it, if it's relevant, or use it as inspiration to create a new one. Ultimately it's giving the typography a personality. A behavior. An outlook. A point of view. An expression.

Can you please explain your design process, touching on any inspirational instructor, design movement or methodology that you draw from?

[LT]My methodology is seeing the world as an oyster. Always being a student and having the thirst to learn. Being open. Wanting to be better without ego. I believe it's important to pay attention. Everything is a source of inspiration. Appreciation for culture, location, history, philosophy, psychology, science, math, theory, spirituality and instinct all play a vital role in my design process.

Now that many brands create video content for online marketing, social media feeds and their own websites, what recommendations would you give new logo designers? Would you recommend that animation play an important role in a logo's design process? If so, what tweaks would you recommend to make a logo better prepared for animation?

[LT]My number one recommendation to new logo designers is not to have an "Art Attack." We are in the business of service. Your job is truly about being a scribe, an interpreter, translator, salesperson and marketer.
It's bringing a vision to life that's born out of a problem that needs to be solved. It's understanding that you have to meet a goal. It's not about your favorite font, color or shape. We live in a world that everyone is visually stimulated at all times. Don't worry that your final design wasn't your favorite. Develop your listening skills and in doing so, you'l learn to ask the right questions. The right question will open the door to a world of possibilities.

Get consumed in building relationships.

Great design comes first. It's truly answering some or all of the who, what, when, where, why and how. I think it's important to forward think about the usage of your logo and know that it will be impacted by the environment that it lives in. By environment I mean print, outdoor, online, billboard display, kiosk, TV, tablet, cell phone, etc.
You should know that it needs to work horizontal, vertical, be legible, scalable, functional and potentially interactive.

Let your static logo be as thoughtful, relevant and as im-pactful as it can be. The animation direction will be the supporting cast to your logo which is the lead.Start by ask-ing yourself, what am I trying to accompish?

Now that many streaming services like Netflix and Hulu are creating their own content, they're pushing the envelope with the motion graphics of their opening se-quences. They're animating type and having it interact much more with the sequence's imagery. Please discuss how this may affect the field of motion graphics.

[**LT**]I believe that it's a continuation of the evolution of de-sign and animation. The beauty of it, is the user, which was formerly either the viewer or consumer, will have a louder voice in the creative process and execution.

It's no longer that we only promote, market and sell to the viewer/consumer in mind. Now the user's taste, behavior, habits, routines, location and interest will play a larger role in how we utilize time and space. How long will those title sequences take to resolve based on attention span needs and wants. What space will the elements have to interact, behave and reveal themselves?

Finally, if you were commissioned to create one of these sequences, what would your design process be? How would you begin?

[**LT**] I would begin by asking the right questions.
I would then draft my version of a creative brief.

Depending on the scale of the project, the brief would have more or less questions. When is this due, time to execute? Budget for design/animation, revisions, etc. The must haves and what should we avoid. What's the goal? Who is this for, the target? Where will it live, the device? How long does it have to be? What music/sound/audio will we be using? Music.sound.audio is the biggest part of animation. It informs how elements respond, react and resolve.
It determines how the user, viewer, consumer will feel.
Prepare mood boards/vision boards or tear sheets. These are visual aids.
Research typography.
After Title is approved then we go onto animation.
Storyboard ideas to client
Once a direction is approved then….
Time to animate…….
I would have my final position locked in time and space.
Then I would take the logo or title and start to separate it.
Then the exploration and inspiration begins to move to the beat of the music and sound in the allowed time.

THE OTHER SIDE

THE OTHER SIDE

THE OTHER SIDE

THE OTHER SIDE

THE OTHER SIDE

206

Jason Cranford Teague

Jason designed the first web-based magazine in 1994 and has been at the forefront of digital innovation ever since. He wrote the first book on CSS for designers in 1998, created the first online graphic novel in 2006, and wrote the first book on modern web typography in 2009. He is a prolific writer (over a dozen books on digital media), speaker (including SXSW, WebVisions, & Internet Summit), and innovation consultant, helping companies small and large with design thinking strategy.

Jason is currently the co-founder and lead creative at InvisibleJets Studio, which is spearheading the drive to bring trust and expertise back online.
Twitter = @JasonCT

Our modern alphabet was created with symbols or icons. As a UI pro, do you see us moving back to iconography? It appears once a decision is made to utilize an icon, it gains popularity and recognition rather quickly, a good example is the hamburger.

[JCT] It would be easy to say "yes." With the growth of emojis, every day it looks as if our syllabic language that requires an alphabet to write is being replaced by modern hieroglyphics. But there is a catch, those hieroglyphics will never be able to convey the complex thoughts that written language using an alphabet can. What a lot of people who bemoan the loss of written communication don't seem to realize is that, although we use emoji and contractions for quick messages, there is an absolute explosion of written language on blogs, message boards, and in social media.

Icons serve an incredibly important purpose to allow us to place specific meaning in a compressed space, but humanity developed syllabic written language because we need to be able to convey complex thoughts, something I don't see going away anytime soon.

What makes you select a typeface for a UI project? What letterform is the key glyph for you?

[**JCT**] For me, it's about memorability and personality. The typeface should visually convey the voice of the client or product. Legibility and readability are actually secondary to that. It's important that the reader not become frustrated reading a font, of course, but there have been some interesting studies into disfluency which indicate that people actually remember information better if they have to work a little harder to read it.

Would you alter an existing font to suit a project?

[**JCT**] Yes, but I would hire an expert to do something like that, which can get expensive. I've priced typefaces for a variety of clients in the past. It's worth it, but difficult to show what the return on investment (ROI) would be for something that esoteric.

Would you consider hand drawing a typeface if a design called for such a treatment?

[**JCT**] Yes, and I have. I experimented with my own hand written font "JasonSpeaking" which I use sometimes in my presentations as a display font. It's fun and it has my personality to it.

What are differences in typography for UI design compared to Way-Finding or print design?

[**JCT**] In many ways they are completely different species. There are the obvious technical differences in how the type is created and displayed which affect how it appears and is consumed by the reader, but to me the biggest difference is the ephemeral nature of type on the screen. Unlike print or signs which are permanent (at least relative to a human life), text on the screen is there one second and gone the next. On the one hand, this gives it a certain disposability that physically rendered text does not have. I think this leads to a very disposable attitude toward textual content on the screen.

Most type layout is done automatically by the computer, so little or no type layout innovation happens online, except on the occasional "experimental" websites. I think this is unfortunate. There is a lot we could do to invigorate type layout online, which could lead to better experiences for the audiences.

How can traditional rules of typography be applied to UI design? If you find that most apply, do you ever break any of them when the effect enhances the end product?

[JCT] I think the problem is that the traditional rules of typography are too easy to apply to UI design, so little time is spent trying to find alternatives. You can set up your CSS rules, and, whoosh, your text is laid out by the book. But that can get pretty boring. We need designers to break the rules more! Use type to communicate ideas in new and interesting ways, which just cannot happen on a Facebook page, or Twitter, or Tumblr, or any cookie cutter design.

Glossary and Resources

Type Terms:

Aperture: The semi-enclosed space created by a curved stroke as seen in letters like C, S and h.

Apex: A letter's top-most point where two angled strokes converge, as seen in the A and M.

Arm/leg: The upper or lower (horizontal or diagonal) stroke that is attached to another stroke on one end, but unconnected on the other. The horizontal strokes on the E and F are good examples.

Bar/crossbar: The horizontal stroke that connects two other strokes, some examples are A, H, R, e, and f.

Bowl: The curvature that creates an enclosed space within a character, the space which is created is in turn named the counter. R's and B's are good examples of letterforms that have bowls.

Counter: A semi- or completely enclosed space inside a character as seen in letters such as R's, B's and d's.

Crotch: The angled negative space created when an arm meets another, or stem. The V is an excellent example of a crotch.

Ear: The small stroke placed in the upper right of the lowercase two story g.

Foot: The part of a character's stem that sits on the baseline.

Hairline: Many typefaces have weight variations, and a hair line is the thinnest stroke within these variations.

Link: The calligraphic stroke that connects the upper and and lower parts of a two-story lower case g.

Loop: Lower half of a two-story lower case g.

Shoulder: The curved stroke as seen in h, m and n.

Spine: The central curved stroke in an S, this is often the thickest stroke in the character.

Spur: The small projection off a main stroke found on many capital G's.

Stem: The straight vertical stroke or the main straight diagonal stroke in a letter as seen in the T and F.

Tail: The additional stroke on the bottom of a Q, or a shortened diagonal stroke of an R.

Terminal: The end of a stroke, which is not completed with a serif.

Links

http://webspace.ship.edu/cgboer/alphabet.html

http://www.templestudy.com/2008/02/17/the-origin-of-the-letter-e/

https://en.wikipedia.org/wiki/List_of_hieroglyphs/Q

http://www.historian.net/hxwrite.htm

http://www.phoenician.org/alphabet.htm

Please visit my website to download many of the vectors that were used in this book's illustrations. The Illustrator files can be found at stephenboss.com.

Bibliography

Naveh, Joseph. *The Early History of the Alphabet An Introduction to West Semitic Epigraphy and Palaeography.* Skokie, Illinois: Varda Books, 2005.

Naveh, Joseph. *Origins of the Alphabet.* London, England: Cassell and Company, 1975.

Sacks, David. *Letter Perfect.* New York, New York: Broadway Books, 2003.

Allenson Picton , James. *The Origin and History of the Numerals, a Paper James Allenson Picton.* The Literary and Philosophical Society of Liverpool, Nov. 30, 1874.

Smith, David E. and Karpinsky, Louis C. *The Hindu-Arabic Numerals.* Boston and London: The Athenæm Press, Boston and London, 1911.

Concise Oxford Dictionary (11th edition revised, 2004).